NOT ALL ROADS
LEAD
TO
HEAVEN
DEVOTIONAL

Also by Dr. Robert Jeffress

Not All Roads Lead to Heaven:
Sharing an Exclusive Jesus in an Inclusive World

A Place Called Heaven:
10 Surprising Truths about Your Eternal Home

Choosing the Extraordinary Life: God's 7 Secrets
for Success and Significance

A Place Called Heaven for Kids: 10 Exciting Things
about Our Forever Home

Courageous: 10 Strategies for Thriving in a Hostile World

A Place Called Heaven Devotional:
100 Days of Living in the Hope of Eternity

Invincible: Conquering the Mountains
That Separate You from the Blessed Life

Encouragement from A Place Called Heaven:
Words of Hope about Your Eternal Home

18 Minutes with Jesus: Straight Talk from the Savior
about the Things That Matter Most

What Every Christian Should Know: 10 Core Beliefs
for Standing Strong in a Shifting World

The 10: How to Live and Love in a World
That Has Lost Its Way

NOT ALL ROADS LEAD TO HEAVEN DEVOTIONAL

100 Daily Readings about
Our Only Hope for Eternal Life

Dr. Robert Jeffress

BakerBooks
a division of Baker Publishing Group
Grand Rapids, Michigan

© 2024 by Robert Jeffress

Published by Baker Books
a division of Baker Publishing Group
Grand Rapids, Michigan
BakerBooks.com

Printed in China

Library of Congress Cataloging-in-Publication Data
Names: Jeffress, Robert, 1955– author.
Title: Not all roads lead to heaven devotional : 100 daily readings about our
   only hope for eternal life / Dr. Robert Jeffress.
Description: Grand Rapids, Michigan : Baker Books, a division of Baker
   Publishing Group, [2024] | Includes bibliographical references.
Identifiers: LCCN 2023010924 | ISBN 9781540903709 (cloth) | ISBN
   9781493444120 (ebook)
Subjects: LCSH: Heaven—Christianity—Prayers and devotions. | Future life—
   Christianity—Prayers and devotions. | Near-death experiences—Religious
   aspects—Christianity—Prayers and devotions.
Classification: LCC BT848 .J39 2024 | DDC 236/.24—dc23/eng/20230526
LC record available at https://lccn.loc.gov/2023010924

Some content in this book has been adapted from Robert Jeffress, *Not All Roads
Lead to Heaven: Sharing an Exclusive Jesus in an Inclusive World* (Grand Rapids:
Baker Books, 2016).

Published in association with Yates & Yates, www.yates2.com.

Baker Publishing Group publications use paper produced from sustainable for-
estry practices and post-consumer waste whenever possible.

24   25   26   27   28   29   30   7   6   5   4   3   2   1

To the faithful supporters of *Pathway to Victory*,
who help us illuminate the only Way to heaven.

DAY 1

Christianity's Most Offensive Belief

The gate is small and the way is narrow that leads to life, and there are few who find it.

—Matthew 7:14

Right now, conservative Christians are waffling and wavering on the foundational belief of Christianity: that salvation is available only through Jesus Christ. A recent Pew survey revealed that 44 percent of American Christians—including almost a fourth of evangelical Christians—say that other religions can lead to eternal life in heaven.[1]

You may say, "As long as I believe in Jesus, what difference does it make if there are other ways to heaven?" The difference it makes is this: what you believe about the exclusivity of Christ for salvation determines whether you spend eternity in heaven or in hell.

7

If you think that's an exaggeration, consider this illustration. Suppose you want to travel to Houston from Dallas. But instead of driving south to Houston, you mistakenly go north to Oklahoma. No matter how sincere you are, if you keep traveling north, you will never get to Houston. You are going the wrong way.

The way to heaven is narrow, and it is only through Jesus Christ.

Jesus said if you want to go to heaven, there's only one way to get there: "Enter through the narrow gate; for the gate is wide and the way is broad that leads to destruction, and there are many who enter through it. For the gate is small and the way is narrow that leads to life, and there are few who find it" (Matt. 7:13–14). The way to heaven is narrow, and it is only through Jesus Christ.

Do you believe that Jesus Christ is the only way to heaven?

Why do you think the exclusivity of Christ for salvation matters?

Lord, thank You for providing a way for me to have eternal life in heaven with You. Help me to stand strong in the belief that salvation comes only through Your Son.

DAY 2

Finding the Right Way to Heaven

How can a man be in the right before God?
—Job 9:2

In Matthew 7:13–14, Jesus said the way to heaven is narrow, and few people find it. He also slammed the door on any possibility of another route to heaven. In John 14:6, He said, "I am the way, and the truth, and the life; no one comes to the Father but through Me."

Let's say you have decided that Jesus is the only way to heaven, and you're trusting in Him, but then you find out Jesus was wrong about that. You discover that in fact there are many roads to heaven. If Jesus is wrong, then He can't be the Son of God, because God knows everything. If Jesus isn't the Son of God, then when He died on the cross, He died for His own sins, not for our sins, and Christianity is false. If Christianity isn't true, then that still doesn't help you determine which road to get on to go to heaven, because there are thousands of religions you can choose from. So if Jesus is wrong, how do you find the right way to heaven?

It's crucial to understand the doctrine of the exclusivity of Christ.

This issue of the exclusivity of Christ is the essence of Job 9:2: "How can a man be in the right before God?" How you answer that question affects not only your eternal destiny but the destiny of your family, your friends, and the entire world. That's why it's crucial to understand the doctrine of the exclusivity of Christ: so that you can stand firm in your beliefs and point the people around you to the only way to heaven.

How does the belief that Jesus is the only way to heaven affect your faith?

How would your faith be different if there were actually many ways to heaven?

Lord, I'm trusting in You for my salvation. Give me opportunities to show other people the only way they, too, can "be in the right" before You.

10

DAY 3

Christians Are Being Outfought

> *The LORD God made garments of skin for Adam and his wife, and clothed them.*
>
> *—Genesis 3:21*

Why are Christians in America losing the battle for the exclusivity of Jesus Christ for salvation? First of all, we're being outfought on the issue of exclusivity. This issue is ground zero for the larger battle between the kingdom of God and the kingdom of Satan. It's the heart of everything God is trying to do and everything Satan is trying to do. The eternal issue for humanity is this: Will you accept God's way of forgiveness through Christ, or will you try to manufacture your own way to God?

Ever since Adam and Eve fell into sin in the garden of Eden, humans have attempted to cover their sin. When

THIS ISSUE IS
GROUND ZERO
FOR THE LARGER
BATTLE BETWEEN
THE KINGDOM
OF GOD AND THE
KINGDOM OF
SATAN.

Adam and Eve sinned, they tried to manufacture their own covering of fig leaves to cover their guilt. That didn't work. God came to them; He killed an animal, took the skin of that animal, and offered it as a covering for Adam and Eve. They had a choice: they could keep their own self-manufactured covering, or they could accept God's covering. That's what the word *atonement* means. It means "covering."

Adam and Eve accepted God's covering for their sin. Later, they had a son named Cain. Cain tried to approach God on his own terms, and God rejected Cain's approach. Every false religion is an adaption of the way of Cain— trying to approach God on your own terms.

The largest issue we face in life is this: Will we follow God's way of salvation, or will we follow our own way?

How have you tried to manufacture your own "covering" for your sin? What was the result?

How does our choice of covering reflect the battle between God and Satan?

God, I'm grateful for the covering You have provided for my sin. Help me to understand the importance of choosing to accept Your way of forgiveness.

DAY 4

Why Satan Loves Religion

The thief comes only to steal and kill and destroy;
I came that they may have life, and have it abundantly.
—John 10:10

Because we were created as spiritual beings, we all have a desire to be reconciled to God, and Satan knows that. That's why Satan doesn't hate religion; he loves religion because it appeals to our desire to be reconciled to God. Satan uses religion to deceive people away from the true way of knowing God.

For example, let's say you are lost in a mountain range at night. But there is a single star illuminating the only way to safety. That's a no-brainer—you follow the light. But suppose instead of one light there are a thousand lights that each illuminate a different path, and 999 of those paths will lead you over a cliff. Suddenly it's much more confusing, isn't it?

It's the same way with the world's religions. Satan uses religion as a false light to lead people away from the true light, Jesus Christ. That's why we cannot underestimate Satan's desire to deceive people away from Jesus Christ. In John 8:44, Jesus said Satan is a liar. In John 10:10, He said Satan "comes only to steal and kill and destroy."

Satan's number one aim is to take as many people to hell as possible, and how is he doing it? By deceiving people into following other religions that turn people away from faith in Jesus Christ alone.

Satan uses religion to deceive people away from the true way of knowing God.

Most people don't understand that we're in a spiritual battle. "Our struggle is not against flesh and blood," Paul said, "but . . . against the spiritual forces of wickedness in the heavenly places" (Eph. 6:12). We are being outfought on the issue of the exclusivity of Christ.

How does Satan use false religion to deceive people?

What can you do to fight back against this deception and point people to the true Light of the World?

Lord, I know we're in a spiritual battle for the message of the gospel. Help me to recognize Satan's schemes and give me the courage to combat his lies with Your truth.

DAY 5

Christians Are Being Outargued

I am not ashamed of the gospel, for it is the power of God for salvation to everyone who believes.

—Romans 1:16

Christians in America are losing the battle about the exclusivity of Christ because, frankly, we are being outargued by the world on this issue.

Sometimes people wonder why I spend time and effort in the secular media. I think about a story I heard from an associate of Jerry Falwell. He said one time he was with Dr. Falwell, who always gave interviews in the secular media, and this interview had been a particularly tough one. After the interview, Dr. Falwell got in the car with this associate, and the associate said, "Dr. Falwell, why do you subject yourself to that? Why do you let people beat up on you in the media like that?"

WE HAVE TO
PRESENT GOD'S
TRUTH BECAUSE
THE CHRISTIAN
MESSAGE IS BEING
DISTORTED BY
THE MEDIA TODAY.

Jerry smiled and said, "Just think about it: I got four minutes to share biblical truth with millions of people, and it didn't cost us a cent to do it." It's always wise to take advantage of those opportunities to share God's truth.

We have to present God's truth because the Christian message is being distorted by the media today. For example, the issue of the sanctity of life has been twisted into a war on women's health. The conviction that marriage should be between one man and one woman has been twisted into hatred and bigotry. The good news that Christ has offered forgiveness to everybody who believes in Him has been twisted into a message of intolerance and condemnation of sincere followers of other faiths. Christians are being outargued, so we have to take advantage of opportunities to share the truth of God's Word.

In what ways have you seen the Christian message being distorted?

How do you take advantage of opportunities to share God's truth instead?

God, it can be frustrating to see Your message distorted by the world. May I take advantage of opportunities to share the truth of Your Word, and may the people around me be receptive.

DAY 6

You Are God's Representative

We are ambassadors for Christ, as though God were making an appeal through us; we beg you on behalf of Christ, be reconciled to God.

—2 Corinthians 5:20

In order for Christians not to be outargued on the issue of the exclusivity of Christ for salvation, we have to take advantage of opportunities to share God's truth.

We have to be willing to argue God's point of view in the public square, but we also have to be equipped to do so. Think about the apostle Paul. When he argued for the gospel, he came armed not just with Scripture but also with compelling reasoning and logic and vivid illustrations to undergird those logical points. And I believe we're going

19

YOU ARE THE FINAL LINK IN A LONG CHAIN OF EVENTS BETWEEN GOD AND ANOTHER PERSON WHO NEEDS TO HEAR THE GOSPEL MESSAGE.

to have to do the same if we're going to win this argument in the public square.

In 2 Corinthians 5:20, Paul said, "We are ambassadors for Christ, as though God were making an appeal through us; we beg you on behalf of Christ, be reconciled to God." God left you and me here for one reason: to be God's mouthpieces in this world. You are the final link in a long chain of events between God and another person who needs to hear the gospel message. And that's why God has left us here: to be His representatives and share His message that Jesus Christ is the only way to receive the gift of eternal life. But if we're going to be effective in that assignment, we have to know what the message is, and we have to be prepared to share that message in the public square.

Are you sometimes hesitant to share God's truth?

What keeps you from taking advantage of opportunities to argue for the Christian message?

Heavenly Father, I know You have called me to be Your representative. Forgive me for being afraid or ashamed, and give me courage to take Your message to those who need to hear it.

DAY 7

Christians Are Being Outmarketed

The god of this world has blinded the minds of the unbelieving so that they might not see the light of the gospel of the glory of Christ.

—*2 Corinthians 4:4*

Not only are Christians being outfought and outargued but we're also being outmarketed on the issue of the exclusivity of Jesus Christ for salvation. In Ephesians 2:2, when Paul described Satan as "the prince of the power of the air," I wonder if he had in mind what Anne Sweeney, former president of Disney-ABC Television Group, referred to as "the most powerful medium in the world"—television.[1]

Television is a very powerful medium. Did you know the average American adult spends three hours a day watching television, and another two and a half hours watching digital video?[2] Think of the messages that are being endlessly pumped into people's minds. When it comes to the issue of spirituality, the message coming from television is antagonistic toward the idea that there's only one way to be saved, and that's through faith in Jesus Christ. And not only television but radio, movies, print, the internet—all spewing forth the lie that there are many ways to God other than faith in Christ.

It's true that Christians are trying to utilize the media as well to voice opposition to that message of inclusivism. We're trying to drown it out, but frankly, it's impossible to drown out. The good news is we don't have to. You see, this battle about the ex-

> *This battle about the exclusivity of Jesus Christ is not an air war; it's a ground war.*

clusivity of Jesus Christ is not an air war; it's a ground war. And the foot soldiers are you and me.

In what ways have you seen the world marketing the lie that there are many ways to heaven?

What can you do to combat this marketing?

Lord, when it seems like the gospel message is being drowned out, help me to remember that Your Word stands forever! Give me the strength to continue spreading Your truth.

DAY 8

The Ground War for the Gospel

[Equip] the saints for the work of service, to the building up of the body of Christ.

—Ephesians 4:12

More than two thousand years ago, Jesus Christ entrusted to twelve people the message that He is the way of salvation. And those twelve took that message and spread it to others, who spread it to others, who spread it to others. And two thousand years later, the message that Christ is the only way to God is still going stronger than ever. This is a ground war, not a war over control of the airwaves. God's plan is to equip people just like you with that message to take to the uttermost parts of the world.

Now, I'm not saying utilizing media isn't important. Our church places a lot of emphasis on television, radio, and the internet, and we're having fantastic results. We are grateful for winning many unbelievers, but the real goal of our ministry is "the equipping of the saints for the work of service, to the building up of the body of Christ" (Eph. 4:12).

God wants you to be equipped. If you're a student, He wants you to be equipped so you can go into that classroom debate and logically present why Christ is the only way to salvation. If you have a job, He wants you to be able to go into that breakroom in your business and have a conversation with other people about the exclusivity of the gospel. He wants you to be able to articulate to that family member or friend why Christ is the only way to be saved. That's God's plan for getting this message out. It's a ground war.

God wants you to be equipped.

Do you feel equipped to share the gospel message and argue God's point of view?

What steps can you take to better prepare yourself?

God, I want to be able to effectively share the message that Jesus is the only way to salvation. Help me to be proactive in becoming a better soldier for Your kingdom.

DAY 9

Compelling Reasoning

The word of God is living and active and sharper than any two-edged sword, and piercing as far as the division of soul and spirit, of both joints and marrow, and able to judge the thoughts and intentions of the heart.

—Hebrews 4:12

God has appointed you and me to be His representatives on earth, sharing the message that Jesus Christ is the only way to heaven. If we're going to be effective in marketing the gospel, then we need to be equipped with compelling reasoning.

In 1 Peter 3:15, the apostle said, "Sanctify Christ as Lord in your hearts, always being ready to make a defense to everyone who asks you to give an account for the hope that is in you, yet with gentleness and reverence." We need to be ready to explain the gospel to anyone who asks us.

How do we get equipped to do that? Well, nothing is more powerful than God's Word. Hebrews 4:12 says, "The word of God is living and active and sharper than any two-edged sword, and piercing as far as the division of soul and spirit, of both joints and marrow, and able to judge the thoughts and intentions of the heart."

But it's not enough to spout off Bible verses to people. Look at the example of Paul. He didn't just quote Bible verses. He used the Word of God, but he also explained the Word of God. Paul presented logical arguments that flowed out of Scripture, and he came up with interesting illustrations to drive home the point that Christ is the only way to be saved. If we are going to be effective foot soldiers for Christ, we need compelling reasoning.

> *If we are going to be effective foot soldiers for Christ, we need compelling reasoning.*

Are you able to explain the gospel to anyone who asks you?

How would you use Scripture to argue for the exclusivity of Christ for salvation?

Lord, Your Word says I need to be ready to give an account for the hope that is in me. Thank You for giving me examples such as the apostle Paul to look to for guidance.

DAY 10

Unwavering Resolve

Brethren, stand firm and hold to the traditions which you were taught.

—2 Thessalonians 2:15

In order to be successful in marketing the gospel message, we need an unwavering resolve. If you're committed to sharing the exclusivity of Christ, don't be surprised at the pressure you will encounter to compromise on this issue.

Back in high school, I was president of the student council. One of my duties was to lead the prayer at the first football game of the season. We were playing a school with a large Jewish population, and the officials pulled me aside and said, "In your prayer, please do not say, 'In Jesus's name.' That would be offensive to many people here tonight." I had dedicated my life to being a pastor, so I thought, *If I'm going to begin my ministry by denying the only name under heaven by which we can be saved, then I don't have any reason being in the ministry.* That night, I prayed with evangelistic fervor. But since that time, I've seen the pressure to compromise on this issue intensify on every Christian.

God has established who can enter heaven.

You've felt that pressure to compromise, haven't you? Christians are being bullied by those outside the faith and badgered by those inside the faith to be more inclusive about the people God allows into heaven. The problem is, we don't have the authority or the ability to do that. God has established who can enter heaven. Jesus said in Matthew 7:14, "The gate is small and the way is narrow that leads to life, and there are few who find it."

Have you felt pressured to be more inclusive about the people God allows into heaven?

How did you respond? What better way could you have responded?

God, it is You—not me or anyone else—who decides who can enter heaven. When I feel pressured to compromise on this issue, give me an unwavering resolve to stand firm on Your truth.

DAY 11

The Temptation of Universalism

The time will come when they will not endure sound doctrine; but . . . they will accumulate for themselves teachers in accordance to their own desires, and will turn away their ears from the truth and will turn aside to myths.

—2 Timothy 4:3–4

Every week, my email inbox is filled with all kinds of interesting questions. Is it all right for Christians to be cremated? Are the six days of creation in Genesis literal twenty-four-hour days? I think you would agree that as intriguing and perhaps even important as those questions are, they're secondary in importance to this question: Are there many ways to get to heaven when you die, or is there only one way to get to heaven?

UNIVERSALISM IS THE BELIEF THAT EVERYBODY GOES TO HEAVEN.

There are four prevalent views today about who will be in heaven. The first of these is *universalism*. Universalism is the belief that everybody goes to heaven. Former pastor Rob Bell popularized this view in his book *Love Wins*. He said, "Millions have been taught that if they don't believe, if they don't accept in the right way, that is, the way the person telling them the gospel does, and they were hit by a car and died later that same day, God would have no choice but to punish them forever in conscious torment in hell. . . . A loving heavenly father who will go to extraordinary lengths to have a relationship with them would, in the blink of an eye, become a cruel, mean, vicious tormenter. . . . That kind of God is simply devastating. Psychologically crushing. We can't bear it."[1]

In other words, universalists say they can't conceive of a God who would send people to hell, and therefore God must not be like that. But that contradicts the truth of Scripture.

Have you ever been tempted to think, *Surely God would never send people to hell*?

How would you respond to someone who feels this way?

What does Scripture say?

Lord, protect me from the temptation to imagine You however I want, rather than as who You are. Remind me of the truth You've revealed in Scripture.

DAY 12

The Appeal of Pluralism

If you confess with your mouth Jesus as Lord, and believe in your heart that God raised Him from the dead, you will be saved.

—Romans 10:9

Are there many ways to get to heaven, or is there only one way? Universalists say that everybody goes to heaven, regardless of what they believe. A second prevalent belief about who goes to heaven is *pluralism*. Pluralism restricts salvation to religious people, regardless of what their religion is. Pluralists maintain that all religions are equally valid. They would say there's a place in hell for drug dealers, murderers, and rapists, but good people—religious people—will go to heaven. They say all religions are like different paths up the same mountain that leads to God.

You can understand why this view is prevalent when you look at the number of people who follow other religions.

According to a Pew Research Center report, in 2017 the world was populated by 1.8 billion Muslims, 1.1 billion Hindus, 500 million Buddhists, and 400 million followers of

Pluralists maintain that all religions are equally valid.

folk religions, in addition to the 2.3 billion people classified as Christians.[1] And you don't have to go to a distant country to find people who subscribe to those other religions—they're likely living right next door to you.

That's why, as this country becomes increasingly diverse, pluralism becomes increasingly popular. Pluralism allows us to send really bad people to hell but it also allows us to let people of all religions into heaven. It doesn't require us saying, "Your religion is wrong." But even though pluralism is appealing, it isn't biblical.

What would you say to somebody who believes that all religions are just different paths to God?

Do you find it difficult to say that someone else's religion is wrong?

God, You have said there's only one way to approach You, not many ways. Help me find the right words to effectively share this truth with the people around me.

DAY 13

The Problem
with Inclusivism

As Moses lifted up the serpent in the wilderness, even
so must the Son of Man be lifted up; so that whoever
believes will in Him have eternal life.

—*John 3:14–15*

Some people answer the question about who will be in
heaven with a third view called *inclusivism*. Inclusivism
holds that the sacrificial death of Christ on the cross is the
only means by which people can be saved—but that a person
can be saved by Christ without personally trusting in Christ.
In other words, people who have never heard the gospel and
simply believe in a revelation of God they see somewhere
in creation go to heaven. And if somebody follows another
religion that's kind of close to Christianity and just calls Jesus
by another name, then that person will go to heaven as well.

IN THE NEW
TESTAMENT,
THERE'S ALWAYS
A LINK BETWEEN
SALVATION
AND PERSONAL
BELIEF.

Inclusivists agree with Peter's statement in Acts 4:12: "There is salvation in no one else; for there is no other name under heaven that has been given among men by which we must be saved." Inclusivists would say, "Amen, I believe that." They believe Christ is the means by which people go to heaven, but they're quick to add that there are people who will be in heaven who have never trusted in Christ. In other words, they say people can receive the gift of salvation without knowing who the sender of the gift is.

Here's the problem with that view: in the New Testament, there's always a link between salvation and personal belief. In fact, you cannot find one example in the New Testament of anybody who was saved without personally trusting in Jesus as Savior.

Have you personally believed in Jesus—and Jesus alone —for your salvation?

If not, when will you make the decision to place your trust in Him?

God, thank You for sending Your Son to die on the cross and save me from my sins. May I put my trust in Christ alone for my salvation and continue to rely on You every day.

DAY 14

The Truth of Exclusivism

Believe in the Lord Jesus, and you will be saved.
—Acts 16:31

Universalism, pluralism, and inclusivism are three popular ways to answer the question of who goes to heaven. But I think the fourth prevalent view of who will be in heaven is also the only biblical view: *exclusivism*. Exclusivism is the belief that salvation is limited to those who exercise personal faith in Jesus Christ. Now, exclusivists say there are two exceptions to that: children who are too young to accept Christ, and people with intellectual disabilities who are incapable of accepting the gospel. We believe they will be in heaven as well.

Many passages in the New Testament connect salvation with personal belief. John 3:16 says, "God so loved the world, that He gave His only begotten Son, that whoever believes in Him shall not perish, but have eternal life." In John 11:25–26,

Jesus said, "I am the resurrection and the life; he who believes in Me will live even if he dies, and everyone who lives and believes in Me will never die." In Acts 16:31, Paul said, "Believe in the Lord Jesus, and you will be saved." There is no salvation apart from a personal belief in Jesus Christ.

The Bible teaches that only those who exercise faith in Christ will be saved.

Now, that raises troubling questions: What about those who have never heard of Jesus? What about those who lived before the time of Jesus? Am I telling you that a good, moral person who sincerely believes in another religion will spend eternity in hell while a serial killer who trusts in Christ as Savior on their deathbed will be in heaven?

God's Word has an answer for every one of those objections. The Bible teaches that only those who exercise faith in Christ will be saved.

What are some questions you've heard (or wondered yourself) about the exclusivity of Christ for salvation?

How does God's Word answer those objections?

Heavenly Father, the world around me is full of wrong beliefs about the way to get to heaven. Help me look to You and Your Word for answers about eternity.

DAY 15

Why Exclusivity Matters

Your word is truth.
  —*John 17:17*

You may wonder, *As long as I trust in Jesus as my Savior, does it really matter if there are different roads that lead to God?* The fact is, if we surrender the doctrine of the exclusivity of Jesus for salvation, there are several other key beliefs we have to surrender as well. Consider a long row of dominoes. When the first domino is toppled, it sets off a chain reaction. Let's imagine the first domino is the belief that Jesus is the only way to be saved. If that first domino falls, other key beliefs are toppled as well.

If we believe there are many ways to be saved, the next domino that falls is the nature of truth. A survey from Dr. George Barna revealed that a majority of evangelical Christians believe there is no absolute moral truth.[1] *Absolute truth* refs to truths that apply to everybody regardless of their culture or the time in which they live.

But many Christians have instead embraced *relativism*, the belief that all truth is conditional based on time and culture. This embracing of relativism explains why so many Christians today support same-sex marriage, practice adultery, and engage in unethical behavior regardless of what the Bible says. They've bought into this idea that we can't say something is right for everybody all the time. But there are some truths that do apply to everybody, including the gospel of Jesus Christ. If we surrender the exclusivity of the gospel, the nature of truth must be surrendered as well.

If we surrender the exclusivity of the gospel, the nature of truth must be surrendered as well.

Why do we have to give up absolute truth if we give up the exclusivity of Christ for salvation?

How would your faith and your life be different if there were no absolute truth?

Lord, thank You for revealing Your truth to me in Your Word. Protect me from the temptation to embrace relativism and help me hold fast to the truth in my attitudes and actions.

DAY 16

The Inspiration of the Bible

Indeed, has God said . . . ?
—Genesis 3:1

If we surrender the doctrine of the exclusivity of Christ for salvation, then we have to give up other important beliefs. The second doctrine we surrender is the nature of truth—if we reject what the Bible says about the exclusivity of Christ, then we can't say that some things are right or wrong for everybody all the time.

The next doctrine we give up—the next domino to fall—is the inspiration of the Bible. Since the beginning of time, Satan has tried to cause us to question whether God's Word can truly be trusted. Remember what the serpent said to Eve? "Indeed, has God said, 'You shall not eat from any tree of the garden'?" (Gen. 3:1). In other words, "Are you sure that's what God said? Are you sure you got it right?"

And that same attack from Satan continues today. He whispers in our ears, "Can you really trust what the Word of God says? Given the abundance of evidence for evolution, has God really said that He formed man out of the dust of the earth? Or given the human body's natural urges, has God really said sex is only to be between a husband and wife? Given the prevalence of different religions in the world, has God really said there is only one way to Him—through faith in Jesus Christ?" If we waffle and waver on the issue of exclusivity, it diminishes the trustworthiness of the Bible.

Since the beginning of time, Satan has tried to cause us to question whether God's Word can truly be trusted.

How does Satan tempt you to doubt the trustworthiness of the Bible?

What can you do to be reassured of the inspiration of God's Word?

Lord, 2 Timothy 3:16 says all Scripture is inspired by You. When I have doubts about the truth of the Bible, strengthen my trust in Your Word.

DAY 17

The Deity of Christ

Everyone who beholds the Son and believes in Him will have eternal life.

—John 6:40

If we surrender the doctrine of the exclusivity of Jesus Christ, then Jesus cannot be the Son of God.

Why does the deity of Christ stand or fall on the exclusivity of the gospel? There are a number of passages in which Jesus said He is the only way to heaven. For example, in Matthew 7:14, Jesus rejected universalism, the idea that everybody's going to heaven. He said, "The gate is small and the way is narrow that leads to life, and there are few who find it."

Jesus slammed the door on pluralism, the idea that all belief systems are equally valid. In John 14:6, He said, "I am the way, and the truth, and the life; no one comes to the Father but through Me."

Jesus also rejected inclusivism, the idea that personal faith isn't necessary to obtain salvation. In John 6:40, He said, "Everyone who beholds the Son and believes in Him will have eternal life." Jesus said He is the only way to heaven, and salvation is only possible through personal faith in Him.

If Jesus was honestly mistaken, then He's not the all-knowing God.

If Jesus was wrong about this, there are only two explanations. First of all, He was honestly mistaken. If Jesus was honestly mistaken, then He's not the all-knowing God. The only other reason Jesus could have been wrong is He was intentionally misleading us—that is, Jesus knew there was more than one way to heaven, but He misled us by saying He was the only way. If He was lying to us, then He couldn't be the perfect Son of God, could He? The deity of Christ rests on this issue.

If Jesus were wrong in claiming to be the only way to heaven, would you still want to follow His example?

Why is it important that Jesus is who He said He is?

God, I believe in the deity of Your Son, who came to earth and lived a perfect life. Help me to follow His example in boldly proclaiming the truth about salvation.

DAY 18

The Necessity of the Cross

*We have an Advocate with the Father, Jesus Christ the
righteous; and He Himself is the propitiation for our sins.*
—*1 John 2:1–2*

A fourth doctrine that falls if we surrender the doctrine of
exclusivity is the necessity of the atonement—that is, the
sacrificial death of Christ for our sins. The cross of Jesus
Christ, that horrific experience of being separated from God,
of experiencing hell for us so that we could have heaven,
wasn't just one way to God; it was the *only* way to God.

If the universalists are right and everybody's going to
heaven, then Jesus's death was unnecessary. If the pluralists are right and religious people are going to heaven, then
Jesus's death was unimportant. The doctrine of the atonement collapses if we believe there's more than one way to
God. God made a tremendous mistake in sending His Son
to die if there is another way to Himself.

GOD MADE
A TREMENDOUS
MISTAKE IN
SENDING HIS SON
TO DIE IF THERE
IS ANOTHER WAY
TO HIMSELF.

Now, most religions say there is a break between God and us that needs to be reconciled. The difference is in how we are reconciled to God. Pagan religions say we have to make sacrifices to appease the angry gods. Eastern religions say we reconcile ourselves to God through self-improvement. Religions like Judaism and Islam say it's by keeping a long list of requirements.

Only Christianity says that we are incapable of satisfying God's requirements, and that only God Himself can offer an acceptable sacrifice. That's why 1 John 2:2 says, "He Himself is the propitiation for our sins." When we trust in Christ for our salvation, we allow the blood of Jesus Christ in some inexplicable way to cover us and forgive all our sins. If the exclusivity of Jesus for salvation isn't true, then the whole idea of Christ dying for our sins collapses.

How does it make you feel to know that Christ went to the cross so that you could go to heaven?

Would your answer change if His death were not the only way to be saved?

Lord, thank You that Jesus loved me so much He was willing to die for me on the cross. May I never devalue His sacrifice by believing it was unnecessary or unimportant.

DAY 19

The Reality of Hell

He who comes from heaven is above all. . . . What He
has seen and heard, of that He testifies.
—John 3:31–32

If we don't believe there's only one way to heaven, then we have to abandon the reality of hell. If universalists are correct and everybody's going to heaven, then no one will be in hell. If pluralists are correct and all religious people are going to heaven, then very few people will go to hell: people like rapists, murderers, and drug dealers. If inclusivists are right and heaven includes the billions of people around the world who have never heard the gospel, then the population of hell is minuscule, right?

That's a contradiction of what Jesus said. If the population of heaven is greater than the population of hell, then hell isn't real because Jesus was a liar and didn't know what He was talking about.

Consider what Jesus said about the population of hell compared to the population of heaven in Matthew 7:13–14: "Enter through the narrow gate; for the gate is wide and the way is broad that leads to destruction, and there are many who enter through it. For the gate is small and the way is narrow that leads to life, and there are few who find it." Jesus said the way to heaven is small. If heaven will have more people in it than hell, then Jesus should have said, "Enter through the wide gate; for the gate is narrow and the way is small (or nonexistent) that leads to destruction." But that's not what Jesus said, is it? If we surrender the exclusivity of Christ, then we have to give up the reality of hell.

Jesus said the way to heaven is small.

What beliefs do you hold about hell? Do those beliefs come from God's Word?

Why does the exclusivity of Christ affect the doctrine of hell?

Lord, sometimes it can be difficult to accept the truth about hell, even though it's in Your Word. Help me to remember the teachings of Jesus as I share with others the reality of heaven and hell.

DAY 20

The Motivation for Missions

Go therefore and make disciples of all the nations.
—Matthew 28:19

If there are ways to God other than faith in Christ, then we might as well give up on evangelism and missions. Christ's final words to His disciples before He ascended into heaven were, "Go therefore and make disciples of all the nations" (Matt. 28:19).

Now, if I had been there at that moment and knew there were other ways to heaven besides faith in Christ, I would've respectfully raised my hand and asked, "Why bother to go into all the world if everybody is going to heaven anyway?" If pluralists are right and all religions are equally valid, why would we risk offending people if their religion is just as good as our religion for getting to heaven? If the inclusivists are right, why would we sacrifice to send people around the world to preach the gospel to those who haven't heard if they would be okay anyway? The only motivation we have for sharing the gospel is that Jesus is the only way to heaven.

The most loving thing we can do is to share the truth.

You and I are God's messengers, and it's time for us to reclaim the gospel from those who would pervert it into a message of hate and instead present it as God intended—as a message of love. The most loving thing we can do is to share the truth: there aren't many ways to God. Every other way is a dead end that leads to eternal separation. There is one way to God through Jesus, who said, "I am the way, and the truth, and the life; no one comes to the Father but through Me" (John 14:6).

What is your motivation for telling other people about Jesus?

How would you explain to a non-Christian why it's important for you to share your faith with them?

Lord, thank You for entrusting me with the task of sharing the gospel with a lost and hurting world. Give me a love for others that compels me to proclaim Your message of salvation.

DAY 21

The Real God

You have ordained Your precepts, that we should keep them diligently.

—Psalm 119:4

David Jeremiah tells an anecdote about a woman who approached him after a service, protesting, "The God I serve would not send people to hell for eternity for not believing in Jesus."

"You're right," he said to the surprised woman. "He wouldn't do that . . . because your god doesn't exist."

Many of us are guilty of serving the god we wish existed instead of the God who actually exists. What's the difference? The difference is eternal life or eternal death.

A. W. Tozer said, "What comes into our minds when we think about God is the most important thing about us."[1] To put a finer point on it, it's very important that when we contemplate God, we aren't thinking about the god who resides in our imagination but instead are thinking about the God who actually rules over all creation. It's important to worship the real God instead of an imaginary god.

If the real God issues certain commands, then those commands are absolute. But if an imaginary god issues commands, those commands are optional. If the real God demands certain things from us, then we'd better do our best to meet His demands. If an imaginary god commands certain things from us and we don't like them, we can just discard the god we don't like and create another imaginary god. If the real God claims there's only one way to worship Him, then we'd better find that one way to approach Him.

It's important to worship the real God instead of an imaginary god.

What comes into your mind when you think about God?

What do you think your ideas about God are based on?

God, I want to worship You, not the god of my own imagination. Please continue to reveal Yourself to Me through Your Word and help me to do what You have commanded me.

54

DAY 22

The Old Way
Was One Way

For whatever was written in earlier times was written
for our instruction, so that through perseverance and the
encouragement of the Scriptures we might have hope.
                                        —*Romans 15:4*

I love the story about the first grader in Sunday school who
was working hard on a drawing. His teacher asked him,
"What are you drawing?"

The kid said, "I'm drawing a picture of God."

The teacher gently explained, "Since no one has seen
God, no one knows what He looks like."

The first grader confidently replied, "They will now!"

While it's true that nobody has seen God the Father, we
do know what God is like. We know what He wants from
us. We know about His likes and dislikes. We know about

His plan and purpose for the universe. How do we know these things about God? They're all recorded in the Bible.

How do we know the Bible can be trusted? We don't have to commit intellectual suicide to believe the Bible is true. There is historical, literary, prophetic, and archaeological evidence that points to the truthfulness of the Bible. We're assuming the fact that the Bible is the Word of God when we say that there aren't many ways to God; there's only one way to God.

The beginning place for finding the truth of the exclusivity of the gospel isn't the New Testament; it's the Old Testament.

The beginning place for finding the truth of the exclusivity of the gospel isn't the New Testament; it's the Old Testament. We're going to discover what the Old Testament has to say about the exclusivity of approaching God in only one way. And as we will see, the old way was truly just one way.

Do you think it's important to study what the Old Testament says about how we approach God? Why or why not?

God, thank You for giving us a Bible we can trust. As I study what the Old Testament says about You, help me to see Your plan for salvation unfolding throughout history.

DAY 23

Is the Old Testament Still Relevant?

These things happened to them as an example, and they were written for our instruction, upon whom the ends of the ages have come.

—1 Corinthians 10:11

You may wonder, "Why does it matter what the Old Testament says about the way to approach God?"

Many people have difficulty knowing how to interpret the Old Testament. The secular media tries to trip me up on this point all the time, asking me, "Why do Christians selectively obey the Bible? You obey some parts and discard other parts of the Bible." Have you ever had people ask you that question? Usually, they're referring to Old Testament commands. They say, for example, "Why do you follow the command in Leviticus 18:22 about homosexual behavior

THE ONLY LAWS WE OBEY FROM THE OLD TESTAMENT ARE THOSE THAT HAVE BEEN REPEATED IN THE NEW TESTAMENT.

but ignore the command in Leviticus 19:19 about wearing two kinds of materials mixed together?"

Now, it's important for you and me to know how to answer that question. Why is one Old Testament command true for today, but one page over we say, "This no longer applies"? Why do we selectively obey the Bible?

The simple answer to that question is this: we don't live under the old agreement. We aren't Jews living in Israel before the time of Christ. We don't obey those laws. The only laws we obey from the Old Testament are those that have been repeated in the New Testament. When we turn to the New Testament, we find prohibitions against adultery, homosexuality, lying, stealing, coveting, and taking the Lord's name in vain. All those Old Testament prohibitions are repeated in the New Testament, and that's how we determine what we are going to obey.

If someone were to ask whether you obey the Old Testament commands, how would you respond?

In what way(s) does the Old Testament affect your life today?

Lord, thank You for giving instructions and examples for how to obey You in Your Word. Help me to do what's pleasing in Your sight and give me wisdom when I am unsure.

DAY 24

The Value of the Old Testament

I, the LORD, do not change.
                    —Malachi 3:6

Before we study what the Old Testament says about how to approach God, it's important to understand the value of the Old Testament. You may be wondering, "If the only parts of the Old Testament that apply to us today are those parts repeated in the New Testament, why read the Old Testament at all?" Believe me, I ask myself that question whenever my read-through-the-Bible program lands me in Leviticus! Why do all those unfamiliar customs and unpronounceable names matter to us in the twenty-first century?

J. I. Packer said the bridge that links the Old Testament with us today is God. He wrote, "It is true that in terms of space, time and culture, [Bible characters] and the historical epoch to which they belonged are a very long way away from us. But the link between them and us is not found at that level. The link is God himself. For the God with whom they had to do is the same God with whom we have to do."[1] Unlike human customs, God does not change. Hebrews 13:8 says God is "the same yesterday and today and forever." The value of the Old Testament is what it teaches us about God Himself.

> *The value of the Old Testament is what it teaches us about God Himself.*

Now, what does this have to do with the exclusivity of Jesus Christ for salvation? Everything. Because when we're talking to people about the way to God, we have to figure out which God we're talking about. You have to make sure that the God you're trying to approach is the God of reality, not the god of your imagination.

What are some things you learn about God in the Old Testament?

Why does the Old Testament matter when it comes to the gospel?

Lord, Your Word says You are the same yesterday, today, and forever. I'm grateful that I can stake my life and my eternity on the firm foundation of a God who never changes.

DAY 25

A False Dichotomy

I and the Father are one.
—John 10:30

The question we should ask ourselves when we read the Old Testament is, *What does this passage teach me about the character of God?*

Unfortunately, many people believe the Old Testament doesn't teach us anything worthwhile—or true—about God. In his book *The God Delusion*, Richard Dawkins wrote, "The God of the Old Testament is arguably the most unpleasant character in all of fiction: jealous and proud of it; a petty, unjust, unforgiving control-freak; a vindictive, bloodthirsty ethnic cleanser; a misogynistic, homophobic, racist, infanticidal, genocidal, filicidal, pestilential, megalomaniacal, sadomasochistic, capriciously malevolent bully."[1]

It isn't only atheists like Dawkins who find the God described in the Old Testament repugnant. Many professing

THERE'S NO
DICHOTOMY
BETWEEN THE
GOD OF THE
OLD TESTAMENT
AND THE JESUS
OF THE NEW
TESTAMENT.

Christians have bought into the false dichotomy between the God of the Old Testament and the God of the New Testament personified in Jesus Christ. When I was a student at a Baptist college, I never will forget hearing my Old Testament religion teacher make this comment: "The Bible is simply a collection of men's ideas about God. In the Old Testament you find man's worst thoughts about God: a bloodthirsty deity who constantly sought revenge. In the New Testament you find man's loftiest ideas of God as exemplified in Jesus." This is a common mindset today among Christians and skeptics alike.

But when you look at the Bible seriously, you'll find there's no dichotomy between the God of the Old Testament and the Jesus of the New Testament. Jesus said Himself in John 10:30, "I and the Father are one."

In what ways does our culture characterize Jesus differently from the God of the Old Testament?

What comes to your own mind when you think about God in the Old Testament and the New Testament?

God, I know that You and Your Son, Jesus Christ, are one. Keep me from listening to what the world says about You instead of what You have revealed about Yourself.

DAY 26

One Bible, One God

The LORD is compassionate and gracious, slow to anger and abounding in lovingkindness.

—*Psalm 103:8*

Many Christians and non-Christians alike have bought into a false dichotomy between the God of the Old Testament and the Jesus of the New Testament. Yet the New Testament doesn't present a one-dimensional God whose only attribute is love. The same Jesus who declared "God so loved the world, that He gave His only begotten Son" (John 3:16) will return in judgment to "strike down the nations, and . . . rule them with a rod of iron [as] He treads the wine press of the fierce wrath of God, the Almighty" (Rev. 19:15).

Similarly, the Old Testament reveals more about God than just His anger against evildoers. From Genesis to Malachi we also find a God who is "compassionate and gracious, slow to anger and abounding in lovingkindness" (Ps. 103:8).

Which God should we listen to and attempt to please: the angry God of the Old Testament, who appears to hate everyone, or the loving God of the New Testament, who judges no one? In the first case, who would want to share the message of a God who is bad-tempered and impossible to please? In the second case, if God is so loving that He accepts everyone as they are, then why bother sharing the gospel since God won't judge people anyway?

God is both loving and just.

In truth, both the Old and New Testament reveal to us a variety of aspects of the same God "with whom we have to do" (Heb. 4:13). God is both loving and just. His righteousness demands that He punish sin, and His love motivates Him to offer a way for sinners to be forgiven.

In what ways does God demonstrate His justice? His love?

How does God's nature reflect the exclusivity of the gospel?

Heavenly Father, thank You for being a God of love and a God of justice. Help me to represent Your nature to the people around me who don't know You.

DAY 27

The Foundational Theme of the Old Testament

Hear, O Israel! The Lord is our God, the Lord is one!
—Deuteronomy 6:4

There's no contradiction between the Old Testament and the New Testament. Just like the New Testament, the Old Testament teaches there are not many ways to the true God; there is only one way. And we see that truth throughout the Old Testament.

What themes of the Old Testament remind us that the old way was one way? The foundational theme of the Old Testament is the oneness of God.

If you were to ask the average Christian today, "What is the most important verse of the Bible?" most Christians would say John 3:16: "For God so loved the world, that He

THE FOUNDATIONAL
THEME OF THE
OLD TESTAMENT
IS THE ONENESS
OF GOD.

gave His only begotten Son, that whoever believes in Him shall not perish, but have eternal life."

But if you were to ask an Israelite living in Old Testament times, "What is the most important verse of the Bible?" they would say Deuteronomy 6:4: "Hear, O Israel! The LORD is our God, the LORD is one!" If they had football games back then, that verse would have been on the banners around the stadium.

Why was that such a foundational verse? As the children of Israel were preparing to enter the promised land, Moses warned that they would be faced with numerous temptations from the pagan Canaanites, as well as all kinds of deities. Moses was saying, "You will be tempted to go after this god and that god, but remember this: God is one. There is one God. There aren't many ways to God; there is one God and one way to that God."

What does it mean to you that "the LORD is one"?

Why is the oneness of God foundational to the entire Bible?

God, when I'm tempted to chase after other gods—whether it's money, a relationship, or the god of my own imagination—help me to remember that You and You alone are God.

DAY 28

The Holiness of God

Holy, Holy, Holy, is the LORD of hosts, the whole earth is full of His glory.

—Isaiah 6:3

If somebody asked your best friend to describe you with one word, what word would they use? Maybe they would say, "Oh, he's *funny*." Does that mean you're funny all the time? No, there are probably times you are serious. You probably don't laugh through that many funerals. Or they might say, "Oh, she's *spontaneous*." Does that mean you're always spontaneous? No, there are probably a few things you plan for as well.

The truth is, there's no single word that describes you entirely. And that would be true about God as well. God has a number of characteristics. He is omnipotent: all-powerful. He's omniscient: all-knowing. He is immutable: unchangeable. These things are true about God all the time. But even though they are true about God all the time, there's no single word that sums up God. God is greater than all His attributes combined, just as you are greater than all your attributes combined.

But if we had to pick a single characteristic of God that transcends all others, it would be the word *holy*. When the prophet Isaiah had a vision of the Lord high and lifted up, he saw angels circling the throne of God and crying out, "Holy, Holy, Holy, is the LORD of hosts, the whole earth is full of His

> *If we had to pick a single characteristic of God that transcends all others, it would be the word* HOLY.

glory" (6:3). It's interesting that the seraphim didn't cry out, "Loving, loving, loving" or "Just, just, just" or "Omnipotent, omnipotent, omnipotent." Instead, the single attribute of God they cried out about was His holiness. Holy, holy, holy.

What one word would you use to describe yourself?

What one word would you choose to describe God?

What does it mean that God is holy?

> *God, there's no way I can adequately describe Your attributes. But I join with the angels in crying, "Holy, Holy, Holy, is the LORD of hosts!"*

DAY 29

God's Holiness Reveals Our Sinfulness

Woe is me, for I am ruined! Because I am a man of unclean lips, and I live among a people of unclean lips.
—Isaiah 6:5

What does the word *holy* mean? In the Bible, the word translated as "holy" comes from a Hebrew word that means "to cut" or "to separate." When we say God is holy, we're saying He is a cut above anyone in heaven or earth. When Isaiah saw the separateness of God, how did he respond? "Woe is me, for I am ruined! Because I am a man of unclean lips, and I live among a people of unclean lips" (Isa. 6:5).

I like the way Mark Buchanan described the experience of Isaiah—and everybody else who truly comes to an awareness of the holiness, the uniqueness, of God. Remember the scene around Isaiah: angels are circling the throne of God, singing, "Holy, Holy, Holy" (v. 3). Buchanan wrote, "Isaiah . . . can't join the song, not yet. His life is being redefined for him. An encounter with God's holiness does that to us: It gives rise, not to song and dance, but to wild, harrowing terror. His holiness is heart-stopping, hair-raising. It scalds and rends and pierces. It elicits from our lips, our unclean lips, no 'Wow!' but 'Woe!'

God's holiness means He is different than we are.

"When we see God, we also see ourselves. When we behold His holiness, we see in that instant our unholiness. His glory reveals our ruin, His purity our vanity, His light our shadows. . . . Before we can ever rest in the holiness of God, first we must be undone by it."[1]

When Isaiah saw the holiness of God, his own sinfulness was brought into sharp relief. God's holiness means He is different than we are.

How do you feel when you think about the holiness of God?

What does God's holiness reveal about you?

Lord, You are different than I am. Help me to see myself and my sinfulness clearly in light of Your holiness. Thank You for covering my sinfulness with the righteousness of Your Son.

DAY 30

God Is Not Like We Are

Your eyes are too pure to approve evil, and You can not look on wickedness with favor.

—Habakkuk 1:13

The true God is different from any other god. Pagan religions picture their gods as participating in evil and even enjoying evil, but Habakkuk said this about the true God: "Your eyes are too pure to approve evil, and You can not look on wickedness with favor" (1:13). Of all the attributes of God, it's His holiness that creates the chasm between God and us—specifically, His zero tolerance level for sin of any kind.

God has zero tolerance for sin. We are so fallen as human beings that we imagine ourselves to be more tolerant, moral, and loving than God is. We say, "Why can't God be accepting of people like we are? We're able to overlook the sin in other people's lives and in our own lives. Why can't God be more like that?"

Our ability to tolerate sin in ourselves and others is not a sign of our godliness; it's a sign of our ungodliness. We're comfortable with sin because we are sinners, but God is absolutely pure and holy, so He has no tolerance for sin of any kind. And it's that zero tolerance for sin that creates distance between God and us.

Our ability to tolerate sin in ourselves and others is not a sign of our godliness; it's a sign of our ungodliness.

God is not like we are. He's the one true God who is holy, who is different, and who can only be approached in one specific way, no matter how sincere our motives. The Old Testament reinforces that there is only one way to God.

Why is repenting of your sins so important? How do you think God views your sin?

Are there sins you have overlooked in your life that you need to repent of?

God, Your Word says You don't tolerate sin of any kind. Help me to have Your perspective on sin, and forgive me for the times I don't live up to Your holy standard.

DAY 31

The Sinfulness of Man

The Lord God called to the man, and said to him, "Where are you?" He said, "I heard the sound of You in the garden, and I was afraid because I was naked; so I hid myself."

—*Genesis 3:9–10*

The fact that God is holy presents a problem for us, because another theme in the Old Testament is the sinfulness of people. There's a moral gulf between holy God and sinful people that began in the garden of Eden and continues today.

John Ortberg vividly illustrated how the everyday choices you and I make demonstrate the depth of that gulf. He wrote, "A businessman on the road checks into a motel room late at night. He knows the kind of movies that are available to him in the room. . . . First he has to say a little prayer: 'Don't look at me, God.'

OUR SINFULNESS SEPARATES US FROM HOLY GOD.

"A mom with an anger problem decides to berate her kids because she's so frustrated. . . . First she has to say a little prayer: 'Don't look at me, God.'

"An executive who's going to pad an expense account—

"An employee who is going to deliberately make a co-worker look bad—

"A student who looks at somebody else's paper during an exam—

"A church member who looks forward to the chance to gossip—

"First must say a little prayer.

"We don't say it out loud, of course. We probably don't admit it even to ourselves. But it's the choice our heart makes:

"*Don't look at me, God.*"[1]

Ever since the garden of Eden, we have tried to hide our sin from God, to find some way to cover over our sin. But God in His holiness can't just look away and pretend not to see our sin. Our sinfulness separates us from holy God.

When have you tried to hide your sin from God? What was the result?

How does our sinfulness affect our relationship with God?

Lord, I know I can't hide my sin from You. May I instead make choices that are pleasing to You, in light of the mercy You have shown me.

The First Act
of Disobedience

> *The serpent said to the woman, "You surely will not
> die! For God knows that in the day you eat from it
> your eyes will be opened, and you will be like God,
> knowing good and evil."*
>
> —*Genesis 3:4–5*

The moral gulf between holy God and sinful people began
in the garden of Eden. God told Adam and Eve, "You can
eat of any tree you want to except one." But Satan utilized a
strategy that he still uses today to deceive people: he caused
Adam and Eve to focus on the one thing God said they
couldn't do instead of all the provisions God made for them.

First, Satan caused them to doubt the word of God, asking, "Indeed, has God said?" (Gen. 3:1). Then he attacked
the character of God, claiming God was trying to rob them

THE MORAL GULF
BETWEEN HOLY
GOD AND SINFUL
PEOPLE BEGAN
IN THE GARDEN
OF EDEN.

of true fulfillment: "God knows that in the day you eat from it your eyes will be opened, and you will be like God, knowing good and evil" (v. 5).

Someone has said that all sin is rooted in contempt for God. In other words, we think God can't be trusted, or He's trying to keep something good out of our lives; therefore, it's up to us to do what's best for us. That is the temptation Satan used in the garden, and it's the same temptation he dangles in front of you and me today.

Unfortunately, Eve took the bait: "When the woman saw that the tree was good for food, and that it was a delight to the eyes, and that the tree was desirable to make one wise, she took from its fruit and ate; and she gave also to her husband with her, and he ate" (v. 6). And that single act of disobedience had eternal consequences.

Do you agree that all sin is rooted in contempt for God? Why or why not?

How is Satan's temptation in the garden of Eden similar to the temptation to reject the exclusivity of Christ?

Lord, examine my heart and root out any contempt for You and Your commandments. Help me to overcome temptation and obey You every day.

81

DAY 33

Our True Spiritual Condition

Through one man sin entered into the world, and death through sin, and so death spread to all men, because all sinned.

—Romans 5:12

Have you ever wondered, "What's the big deal about Adam and Eve's sin?" In Romans 5:12, Paul explained what that one act of disobedience means to us: "Through one man sin entered into the world, and death through sin, and so death spread to all men, because all sinned." Because of Adam and Eve's disobedience, sin spread like a virus through the entire human race, and with sin came death—spiritual separation from God.

Every hour of every day we prove that we have inherited the sin virus, don't we? G. K. Chesterton wrote, "Original

EVERY HOUR
OF EVERY DAY
WE PROVE
THAT WE HAVE
INHERITED THE
SIN VIRUS.

sin . . . is the only part of Christian theology which can really be proved" because we "can see [it] in the street."[1]

You might say, "Well, I'm not that bad." Here's the problem with that conclusion: you and I aren't qualified to diagnose our spiritual condition. Some years ago, I had a biopsy on a polyp. I could have dismissed it and said, "It's just a small polyp. No big deal." But that diagnosis would've been meaningless because I'm not a doctor and therefore am not qualified to know the true state of my health.

Unfortunately, God has performed a biopsy of the human condition, and the results are not good. Here's what He's written on our "chart": "The LORD saw that the wickedness of man was great on the earth, and that every intent of the thoughts of his heart was only evil continually" (Gen. 6:5). We have a malignancy on our souls that leads to eternal death. That's why Adam and Eve's sin was a big deal.

What evidence do you see that we have inherited the sin virus from Adam and Eve?

How does our sinfulness affect the way we approach God?

Lord, I can't help but be saddened by the brokenness I see in the world around me. I look forward to the day when all creation will be redeemed from the power of sin and death. Come, Lord Jesus!

DAY 34

The Total Depravity of Man

*They are corrupt, they have committed abominable
deeds; there is no one who does good.*

—*Psalm 14:1*

Theologians call the sinful human condition "total depravity." We wince at that because it hurts our pride to say we're
totally depraved. We look around and say, "There are non-
Christians who do good things. How can we say that people
are totally depraved?"

Total depravity doesn't deal with the *depth* of our sin
but the *breadth* of our sin. Total depravity means that sin
has spread to every part of our lives. Every part of our lives
has been infected and polluted by sin. Our sin has pulled
us away from God.

We have a hard time understanding the great distance
between sinful people and holy God when we use the wrong

EVERY PART OF OUR LIVES HAS BEEN INFECTED AND POLLUTED BY SIN.

standard by which to judge ourselves. It's human nature to compare ourselves to people we think are worse than we are. We say, "Compared to Adolf Hitler or Osama bin Laden, I'm a pretty good person." But that's the wrong standard. When God evaluates us, He doesn't compare us to other people; He compares us to Himself. And by that standard, we are totally depraved.

Think of it this way: the difference between the North Pole and South Pole is considerable, but that difference is negligible compared to the distance between the North Pole and the farthest star in the universe. So it is in our relationship with God. We think there's a great difference between human beings. But the difference between people is negligible compared to the distance between us and God.

Have you ever thought, *I'm a pretty good person. I'm certainly not as bad as so-and-so*?

Why is it dangerous to judge ourselves by comparing our sinfulness to that of other people?

Lord, help me not to think more highly of myself than I ought to think, as Paul wrote, but to be grateful for Your grace. Thank You for reaching across the distance between us to offer salvation.

DAY 35

The Need for a Sacrifice

The LORD God made garments of skin for Adam and his wife, and clothed them.

—Genesis 3:21

Because we are sinners and God is holy, we need a sacrifice for our sin. We see that in Genesis 3:7 after Adam and Eve rebelled against God: "The eyes of both of them were opened, and they knew that they were naked; and they sewed fig leaves together and made themselves loin coverings." Sin always produces guilt, and guilt produces a desire to cover over our guilt. That's what Adam and Eve did. They tried to sew their own cover to hide their nakedness.

But notice what happened in verse 8: "They heard the sound of the LORD God walking in the garden in the cool of the day, and the man and his wife hid themselves from the presence of the LORD God." In the coolest part of the day, Adam and Eve started to feel a little drafty. They were aware of how inadequate their covering was. That's the moment God confronted them, and only after God confronted them were they in a position to receive the covering He had made: "The LORD God made garments of skin for Adam and his wife, and clothed them" (v. 21).

Something innocent must die for the guilty to cover our sin.

The very first recorded death in the Bible was an animal God killed to provide a covering for Adam and Eve. God was teaching them the most important lesson we can learn, which is this: something innocent must die for the guilty to cover our sin, and God is the one who provides the sacrifice.

Why did Adam and Eve try to hide their guilt from God?

At what point were they ready to receive God's covering for their sins?

God, I know any covering I try to make for my sin is inadequate. May I be grateful continually for the sacrifice You provided to cover my sin.

DAY 36

The Provider of the Sacrifice

The life of the flesh is in the blood, and I have given it to you on the altar to make an atonement for your souls.

—Leviticus 17:11

We see the need for a sacrifice throughout the Old Testament. For example, the highest day on the Jewish calendar was the Day of Atonement. That was the one day a year the high priest could enter the Holy of Holies, where the ark of the covenant was kept. The lid of the ark was called the mercy seat, and that's where God's presence was thought to dwell. Inside the ark was a copy of the Ten Commandments. The picture was clear: God was literally looking down at the law. His people had broken it, and so judgment was necessary.

But on the Day of Atonement, according to Leviticus 16, the high priest would first make a sacrifice for his own sins. Then he would kill a goat, enter the Holy of Holies, and place the blood on the mercy seat. The picture was that God no longer saw their lawbreaking; instead, He saw the blood covering over the sins of the people. That was the lesson God was teaching: something innocent had to die for the guilty.

We see the need for a sacrifice throughout the Old Testament.

Who created the sacrifice? Did the Israelites create the goat that was offered to atone for their sins? No. God said in Leviticus 17:11, "The life of the flesh is in the blood, and I have given it to you on the altar to make an atonement for your souls." God created the sacrifice.

If you had to explain to somebody why we need a sacrifice to cover our sin, what would you say?

Why is it important that God is the one who provides the sacrifice?

Lord, Your Word illustrates our need for a sacrifice and Your provision of the sacrifice. Help me to understand this narrative of Your justice and mercy so that I may explain it to others.

DAY 37

A Superior Sacrifice

Through His own blood, He entered the holy place once for all, having obtained eternal redemption.

—*Hebrews 9:12*

In Genesis 22:2, God said to Abraham, "Take now your son, your only son, whom you love, Isaac, and go to the land of Moriah, and offer him there as a burnt offering." Abraham obeyed God and took Isaac up to Mount Moriah, and Isaac willingly submitted himself to be put on the altar. But as Abraham raised the knife to kill his son, "the angel of the LORD called to him from heaven and said, 'Abraham, Abraham! . . . Do not stretch out your hand against the lad'" (vv. 11–12). Abraham looked over and saw a ram caught in the thicket. God had provided the ram to be sacrificed instead.

It's no accident that in that same region called Moriah—which literally means "God will provide"—two thousand years later, another sacrifice was offered: the Lamb of God who takes away the sin of the world. God was teaching us the lesson that someone innocent must die for those of us who are guilty, and God is the one who provides the sacrifice.

In the Old Testament, a sacrifice had to be offered year after year to atone for the sins of the people. But look at what Jesus did for us: "When Christ appeared as a high priest of the good things to come, He entered through the greater and more perfect tabernacle, not made with hands, that is to say, not of this creation; and not through the blood of goats and calves, but through His own blood, He entered the holy place once for all, having obtained eternal redemption" (Heb. 9:11–12). Christ is the one who has offered the sacrifice for our sins.

Christ is the one who has offered the sacrifice for our sins.

Why is it significant that Jesus offered Himself as a sacrifice?

Would His sacrifice matter if there were other ways to be saved from sin?

Heavenly Father, thank You for sending Your Son as a once-for-all sacrifice to redeem me from the power of sin and death.

93

DAY 38

The Exclusivity of the Sacrifice

You are to perform My judgments and keep My statutes,
to live in accord with them; I am the LORD your God.
So you shall keep My statutes and My judgments, by
which a man may live if he does them; I am the LORD.
—*Leviticus 18:4–5*

We need a sacrifice to cover over our sin. And a main theme throughout the Old Testament is the exclusivity of the sacrifice.

As you read through the Old Testament, you'll find over and over again the specificity with which God gave instructions. For example, when God told Noah to build an ark in Genesis 6, did He say, "Just use your creativity—build the boat any way you want to"? No, God gave Noah a blueprint of exactly how He wanted that ark built. He was very specific in His instructions.

Or think about when God gave Moses instructions for the construction of the tabernacle in Exodus 25–31. Did He say, "Just build whatever you want"? No, every detail was given by God, down to the hem on the garment that the priest would wear.

And when God gave the Israelites instructions about offerings in Leviticus 16–27, did He say, "Just offer anything you want to offer to Me. I'm not interested in the details; all I care about is the condition of your heart"? No, God gave specific directions about each kind of offering and how it was to be presented to the Lord.

We have to approach God on His terms, not on our terms.

The truth is, we have to approach God on His terms, not on our terms. That's the message we find over and over again in the Old Testament.

Have you ever given instructions that weren't followed? What was the result?

How did you feel?

Why do you think God is so specific in His instructions?

God, thank You for providing specific instructions for how to approach You. Help me to be uncompromising in telling people the way of salvation You have prescribed.

DAY 39

Beware the Way of Cain

By faith Abel offered to God a better sacrifice than Cain.
—Hebrews 11:4

Perhaps the best illustration of how we approach God is the story of Cain and Abel, the children of Adam and Eve. Genesis 4:3–5 says, "Cain brought an offering to the Lord of the fruit of the ground. Abel, on his part also brought of the firstlings of his flock and of their fat portions. And the LORD had regard for Abel and for his offering; but for Cain and for his offering He had no regard."

Why did God accept Abel's offering and reject Cain's offering? Hebrews 11:4 tells us: "By faith Abel offered to God a better sacrifice than Cain, through which he obtained the testimony that he was righteous." I believe God gave very specific instructions to Cain and Abel about the gifts they were to give. Undoubtedly, God required an animal sacrifice to remind Cain and Abel of their need for God's forgiveness.

How did they treat those instructions? Abel obeyed and brought an animal, but Cain brought grain and fruit. Cain tried to come to God on his own terms rather than God's terms. The New Testament writer Jude asserted that Cain's act of disobedience was the genesis of every false religion in the world today: "Woe to them! For they have gone the way of Cain" (v. 11). The way of Cain represents every religion that tries to approach God in its own way other than through Jesus Christ. True faith in Jesus Christ says there's one way to approach God. Beware those who follow the way of Cain.

> *The way of Cain represents every religion that tries to approach God in its own way other than through Jesus Christ.*

What did Cain's and Abel's offerings say about their regard for God?

What does our own obedience or disobedience say about our regard for God?

Lord, I want to demonstrate my love for You. Grant me the desire to obey Your commandments and the strength to reject those things in my life that displease You.

DAY 40

Characteristics
of the Way of Cain

Woe to them! For they have gone the way of Cain.
—Jude 11

Did you know there are not really thousands of religions in the world today? There are only two: the true religion, which says there's one way to approach God and that's through faith in Jesus Christ, and the way of Cain, which says anyone can come to God in their own way. The way of Cain represents the thousands of religions that try to approach God on their own terms rather than on God's terms.

What is the way of Cain? Let's look at six characteristics:

1. The way of Cain refers to any individual who attempts to approach God on his or her own terms rather than on God's terms.

2. The way of Cain describes any religious system that attempts to earn God's favor by works and rituals rather than by reliance on God's grace.

3. The way of Cain is any religious system that appeals to our pride rather than our desperate condition before God.

4. The way of Cain emphasizes humanity's goodness rather than humanity's sinfulness.

5. The way of Cain says there are many paths that lead to God rather than one path.

6. The way of Cain leads to eternal death rather than eternal life. Proverbs 14:12 says, "There is a way which seems right to a man, but its end is the way of death."

What are some examples of people following the way of Cain that you see around you?

Why do you think the way of Cain appeals to people?

Lord, Your Word says Satan deceives people into following the wrong path. Help me to avoid the way of Cain and give me the discernment to recognize when others are on the wrong path to You.

DAY 41

The Danger of
the Wrong Approach

*There is a way which seems right to a man, but its end
is the way of death.*

—Proverbs 14:12

We naturally rebel against this idea of exclusivity, that
there's only one way to approach God. We tend to think that
somehow spiritual laws are less exacting than the physical
laws that govern the world we can see around us. But if we
make that conclusion, we are in real danger.

On August 2, 1985, Delta Airlines Flight 191 was making its final approach to runway 17L at Dallas–Fort Worth
International Airport. There was bad weather in the area,
and a rainstorm had formed in the path of the jetliner's
descent. Instead of going around that storm, the crew decided to fly through it. What they didn't realize was that

THERE ARE INVISIBLE BUT VERY REAL SPIRITUAL LAWS THAT GOVERN OUR APPROACH TO GOD.

within that storm, there were invisible but very real forces at work for which their jetliner was no match. The storm produced a "microburst"—a violent downdraft that slams straight into the ground, causing hurricane-force winds to spread out in all directions like a starburst. Those invisible winds grabbed hold of the jetliner and caused it to crash, taking the lives of 137 people.[1]

Just as there are natural laws of aerodynamics and physics that governed the course of that jetliner, so there are invisible but very real spiritual laws that govern our approach to God. We can say, "I'll approach God in my way," but the result will be spiritual disaster. There are not many ways to God; there is one way to approach God. It is through Jesus Christ, who said, "I am the way, and the truth, and the life; no one comes to the Father but through Me" (John 14:6).

What are some laws or forces that affect your daily life?

What happens if you try to circumvent those laws or forces?

Lord, remind me that Your laws are real even though they're invisible. Help me to submit to Your laws and to see Your hand moving in the world and in my life.

DAY 42

The Intolerant Christ

Jesus entered the temple and drove out all those who were buying and selling in the temple, and overturned the tables of the money changers and the seats of those who were selling doves.

—Matthew 21:12

When you hear the name Jesus, what's the first word that comes to your mind? You might say *gentle*, *loving*, or *compassionate*. But I imagine there's one word that isn't on your list. It's the word *intolerant*. To describe the Son of God as intolerant borders on blasphemy, we think. But the reason that's true is we have confused the Jesus of our imagination with the Jesus who actually exists.

Contrary to most people's opinion, Jesus wasn't a wimpy rabbi who roamed the countryside plucking daisies and saying nice things to people. That's what most of the world thinks about Jesus. Dorothy Sayers contrasted the Jesus of

WE HAVE
CONFUSED
THE JESUS OF
THE BIBLE
WITH THE
JESUS OF OUR
IMAGINATION.

most people's thinking with the Jesus who actually exists. She wrote, "We have very efficiently pared the claws of the Lion of Judah, certified him 'meek and mild,' and recommended him as a fitting household pet for pale curates and pious old ladies. . . . We cannot blink at the fact that gentle Jesus, meek and mild, was so stiff in his opinions and so inflammatory in his language that he was thrown out of church, stoned, hunted from place to place, and finally gibbeted as a firebrand and a public danger."[1]

There's a popular image on social media of Jesus driving the money changers out of the temple, and the caption says, "If anyone ever asks you 'What would Jesus do?' remind them that flipping over tables and chasing people with a whip is within the realm of possibilities." We have confused the Jesus of the Bible with the Jesus of our imagination.

How do you think Jesus is perceived by the world at large?

How does the world's view of Jesus differ from the Jesus of the Bible?

Lord, I want to model my attitudes, actions, and affections after Your Son—not the Jesus of my imagination but the Jesus of the Bible. Help me to look to His example.

DAY 43

What Jesus Taught about His Uniqueness

He who has seen Me has seen the Father.
—John 14:9

When it comes to salvation, it's critical that we base our beliefs on what Jesus actually said instead of what we wish He had said. For example, Jesus claimed to be God. When Jesus lived, the Gentiles ruled the world. And the Gentiles, specifically the Romans, believed in a multitude of gods. Yet against that background, Jesus said, "I am the one true God." To the Jews, Jesus said, "I am the God your forefathers worshiped in the Old Testament."

Perhaps you've heard a myth that's been around for ages. This myth says Jesus Himself never really claimed to be God; rather that was something His followers claimed about Him long after He'd died. The problem with this idea

WHEN IT COMES TO SALVATION, IT'S CRITICAL THAT WE BASE OUR BELIEFS ON WHAT JESUS ACTUALLY SAID INSTEAD OF WHAT WE WISH HE HAD SAID.

is it doesn't coincide with historical fact. Over and over again, Jesus claimed to be God. In John 10:30, Jesus said, "I and the Father are one." In John 14:9, He said, "He who has seen Me has seen the Father."

Isn't it interesting that none of the founders of any other major religions ever claimed to be God? Buddha never claimed to be God. Confucius never claimed to be God. Mohammed never claimed to be God. Only Jesus claimed to be God. And He not only made that claim but proved it was true by what He did. Jesus claimed He could heal the sick, and He did. He claimed He could rise again from the dead, and He did. Jesus claimed to be God. That's what made Him unique.

Where do you think people get their information about Jesus?

What can you do to help the people around you learn what Jesus actually said and did?

Heavenly Father, thank You for sending Your Son to be a living expression of You here on earth. May I be bold in helping others to understand who Jesus is and who He isn't.

DAY 44

Jesus Claimed to Be God

Jesus said to them, "Truly, truly, I say to you, before Abraham was born, I am."

—John 8:58

Throughout the Gospels, Jesus claimed to be God. Consider Jesus's words to a group of Jews in John 8:51: "Truly, truly, I say to you, if anyone keeps My word he will never see death." They responded, "Surely You are not greater than our father Abraham, who died? The prophets died too; whom do You make Yourself out to be?" (v. 53). In other words, "Everybody dies! Even Abraham, the father of our nation, died. So did all the prophets. Just who do You think You are, Jesus?"

Jesus said, "Your father Abraham rejoiced to see My day, and he saw it and was glad" (v. 56). Now the Jews were really confused. Jesus wasn't even fifty years old. How could He have had any relationship with Abraham? Look how Jesus answered: "Truly, truly, I say to you, before Abraham was born, I am" (v. 58). That set off alarm bells in the Jews' minds.

Throughout the Gospels, Jesus claimed to be God.

The phrase "I am" is the most holy name for God—Yahweh. It was the name God identified Himself by when He appeared in the burning bush. He said to Moses, "I AM WHO I AM. . . . Thus you shall say to the sons of Israel, 'I AM has sent me to you'" (Exod. 3:14). Jesus was using that same phrase, "I am," to identify Himself.

The Jews clearly understood what Jesus was claiming. Look at their response: "Therefore they picked up stones to throw at Him" (John 8:59). Jesus was saying, "I am God."

If somebody told you Jesus never claimed to be God, how would you respond?

Why do people have mistaken ideas about Jesus?

God, Your name is sacred. Thank You for sharing it with us and for revealing Yourself to us through Jesus.

DAY 45

Why Jesus Was Crucified

Unless you believe that I am He, you will die in your sins.
—John 8:24

The night before He was crucified, Jesus was arrested and tried before Caiaphas, the high priest. He asked Jesus, "Are You the Christ, the Son of the Blessed One?" (Mark 14:61). Jesus answered, "I am" (v. 62). Jesus could have stopped there, but He drove His point home by adding, "and you shall see the Son of Man sitting at the right hand of Power, and coming with the clouds of heaven" (v. 62). Jesus was quoting Daniel 7:13, which prophesied the Messiah's second coming. By quoting that verse about Himself, Jesus was saying to Caiaphas, "You think you're the big cheese right now, but one day you're going to see Me coming with power. Your authority on earth is limited, but Mine is eternal."

Look at how Caiaphas reacted: "Tearing his clothes, the high priest said, 'What further need do we have of witnesses?

You have heard the blasphemy; how does it seem to you?' And they all condemned Him to be deserving of death" (vv. 63–64). Jesus didn't get crucified for telling people to turn the other cheek but for claiming to be the Son of God.

Jesus also claimed that belief in Him leads to eternal life. In John 6:40, He said, "Everyone who beholds the Son and believes in Him will have eternal life." What about those who don't believe in Him? Jesus said in John 8:24, "Unless you believe that I am He, you will die in your sins." Notice Jesus didn't say, "Whoever sincerely follows the god of his or her own choosing has eternal life." No, He said, "Only those who believe in Me have eternal life."

> *Jesus also claimed that belief in Him leads to eternal life.*

Why was Jesus crucified?

How do you think the average person would answer that question?

What does the crucifixion say about Jesus's identity?

Lord, I believe in what Jesus Christ did for me on the cross. Give me a longing for the day when He will return with power to establish His kingdom.

DAY 46

What Jesus Taught about His Death

No one has taken [My life] away from Me, but I lay it down on My own initiative.

—John 10:18

Some people think Jesus's death was a tragic end to an otherwise happy story. They picture Jesus traveling around the countryside with His disciples, teaching and doing all these wonderful things, until some bad men grabbed hold of Him and nailed Him to a cross. What a tragedy!

But Jesus said, "I lay down My life so that I may take it again. No one has taken it away from Me, but I lay it down on My own initiative" (John 10:17–18). That was His whole reason for coming to earth: to lay down His life.

Jesus repeatedly taught that His death was central to His mission. For example, Matthew 16:21 says, "From that time Jesus began to show His disciples that He must go to Jerusalem, and suffer many things from the elders and chief priests and scribes, and be killed, and be raised up on the third day." Jesus was telling His disciples that His upcoming crucifixion and resurrection were part of the plan. And He said in John 12, "Now My soul has become troubled; and what shall I say, 'Father, save Me from this hour'? But for this purpose I came to this hour. . . . And I, if I am lifted up from the earth, will draw all men to Myself." But He was saying this to indicate the kind of death by which He was to die" (vv. 27, 32–33). Jesus's death wasn't some unforeseen, unfortunate tragedy; it was central to His mission.

> *Jesus's death wasn't some unforeseen, unfortunate tragedy; it was central to His mission.*

What was Jesus's reason for coming to earth? How would the message of the gospel be different if Jesus's death were not planned?

Heavenly Father, it amazes me to think that Jesus came to earth knowing He would die for my sins. Help me never to forget the enormity of what You have done for me.

DAY 47

The Payment for Our Sins

He said, "It is finished!" And He bowed His head and gave up His spirit.

—John 19:30

Jesus taught that His death on the cross was central to His mission. So what did it accomplish? Jesus's death was payment for our sin debt.

The Bible says every time you and I sin, we go into debt to God. Every time we have an ungodly thought or engage in an ungodly action, that debt we owe to God piles up higher and higher. What happens when we die? Jesus said in John 8:24, "Unless you believe that I am He, you will die in your sins." Do you know what it means to "die in your sins"? It means to die without your debt having been paid.

You see, the biggest decision we make in life is how we're going to pay for our sins. We can say, "I'll pay off the debt myself." But the fact is, you and I owe God a debt we could never repay. If we choose to pay off our sin debt ourselves, then we'll spend eternity in hell trying to do so.

Jesus paid our sin debt for us, but He doesn't force us to accept that payment.

Our other choice is to let Jesus's death pay for our sins. When Jesus hung on the cross, He said, "It is finished!"—literally, "paid in full" (John 19:30). Jesus paid our sin debt for us, but He doesn't force us to accept that payment. We get to choose how we're going to pay for our sins. We can pay for it, or we can let Christ pay for it.

Have you or someone you know ever been deep in debt?

How would you feel if someone offered to completely pay off a debt you owed?

Lord, I know my sins put me in debt to You. May I feel the relief of Your forgiveness that David expressed in Psalm 32:2: "How blessed is the man to whom the LORD does not impute iniquity!"

DAY 48

The Ransom for
Our Freedom

*The Son of Man did not come to be served, but to serve,
and to give His life a ransom for many.*
> —Matthew 20:28

Jesus's death wasn't only the payment for our sins but also
the ransom for our freedom. In Matthew 20:28, Jesus said,
"The Son of Man did not come to be served, but to serve,
and to give His life a ransom for many." The word translated
"ransom" described a payment that was made for a slave or
a prisoner to purchase their freedom.

You and I are born into this world slaves of Satan. He's a
cruel taskmaster, but Jesus paid the price to buy our freedom. He ransomed us out of the ownership of sin and death
and brought us into His own presence.

He didn't purchase your freedom to set you free to live however you want to live. Paul said, "Do you not know . . . that you are not your own? For you have been bought with a price" (1 Cor. 6:19–20). Salvation isn't the freedom to do what we want to do; it's the freedom to do what Christ wants us to do. He purchased us with His own blood. That's why Jesus came—to be a ransom for our freedom.

Jesus paid the price to buy our freedom. He ransomed us out of the ownership of sin and death.

The only way Jesus could pay our sin debt and ransom us from the clutches of Satan was by His own death. If there was any other way, then the death of Jesus was unnecessary. But there was no other way. That's the reason He came.

How does knowing Jesus paid a high price to secure your freedom change your perspective on the way you live your life?

What specific changes are you inspired to make?

Lord, I'm so grateful You paid the ultimate price to free me from sin and death. May I honor Jesus's sacrifice with my life, knowing I am not my own.

DAY 49

What Jesus Taught about Eternity

These will go away into eternal punishment, but the righteous into eternal life.

—Matthew 25:46

What happens to those who fail to follow Jesus? What about those who try to find another path to God? Will they make it to heaven? Let's look at what Jesus had to say about eternity.

First, Jesus taught that two eternal destinations exist. Universalists claim that everyone's going to heaven regardless of what they believe. But Jesus drove a stake through that claim when He said in Matthew 25:46, "These will go away into eternal punishment, but the righteous into eternal life." Jesus taught there are two destinations: eternal punishment and eternal life.

HELL IS A REAL DESTINATION, AND IT'S A PERMANENT DESTINATION.

Second, Jesus taught that hell is a reality. Do you realize that of all the verses in the New Testament that record the words of Jesus, 13 percent deal with the reality of hell? For example, Jesus believed that hell is an actual location, not a state of mind (Matt. 25:46). Jesus taught in Matthew 22:13 that hell is a place of physical suffering. And most devastatingly, Jesus said that hell is an irrevocable destination. Once there, no one leaves. In Luke 16, Jesus told the story about a rich man, a poor man named Lazarus, and Abraham. The rich man found himself in hell and begged Abraham to provide relief and a way out. Abraham answered and said, "Between us and you there is a great chasm fixed, so that those who wish to come over from here to you will not be able, and that none may cross over from there to us" (v. 26). Hell is a real destination, and it's a permanent destination.

Why do you think Jesus talked so much about hell?

What are some misconceptions people have about hell?

God, if I truly believe what Jesus said about hell, then I ought to feel an urgency about sharing the gospel. May the reality of hell motivate me to tell people about the only way of salvation.

DAY 50

What Jesus Taught about the Necessity of Personal Faith

I am the resurrection and the life; he who believes in Me will live even if he dies, and everyone who lives and believes in Me will never die. Do you believe this?

—John 11:25–26

To reject what Jesus taught about heaven and hell means you have to reject Jesus Christ Himself. He taught that hell is a reality, and in Matthew 7:13–14, He said the majority of people will spend eternity there. Similarly, Jesus rejected the claim that everybody is going to heaven because of what His death accomplished. The inclusivist says it's true that Jesus Christ's death made it possible for people to go to heaven, but His death applies to everyone regardless of what they believe.

To REJECT WHAT
JESUS TAUGHT
ABOUT HEAVEN
AND HELL
MEANS YOU
HAVE TO REJECT
JESUS CHRIST
HIMSELF.

But Jesus repeatedly said personal faith is a requirement for heaven. For example, in John 5:24, He said, "He who hears My word, and believes Him who sent Me, has eternal life, and does not come into judgment, but has passed out of death into life."

In John 6:40, He said, "This is the will of My Father, that everyone who beholds the Son and believes in Him will have eternal life, and I Myself will raise him up on the last day."

And in John 11:25–26, Jesus said to His friend Martha, "I am the resurrection and the life; he who believes in Me will live even if he dies, and everyone who lives and believes in Me will never die." And then He asked Martha a question that is important for each of us to answer today: "Do you believe this?"

Over and over again, Jesus said belief in Him is the link to eternal life.

Are there some things Jesus said that you don't believe but other things you do? How do you decide which to believe?

If Jesus is not the only way to be saved, why did He say He was?

Lord, You made it clear in Your Word that personal faith is a requirement to enter heaven. I pray the words of the father in Mark 9:24: "I do believe; help my unbelief."

DAY 51

What It Means to Believe

> *[The unclean spirit] cried out, saying, "What business do we have with each other, Jesus of Nazareth? Have you come to destroy us? I know who You are—the Holy One of God!"*
>
> —Mark 1:23–24

Jesus repeatedly taught that belief in Him is required to spend eternity in heaven. What does it mean to believe in Jesus? It doesn't mean to agree intellectually to a certain set of facts about Jesus. People say, "I believe Jesus is the Son of God. I believe He died for the sins of the world. I believe He rose again on the third day." Guess what? You can believe all those things and still split hell wide open when you die. Satan and his demons believe all those things too—in fact, they believe them more than you do because they were there. They did everything they could to prevent Jesus from going to the cross because they knew what His death would accomplish.

JESUS REPEATEDLY
TAUGHT THAT
BELIEF IN HIM
IS REQUIRED TO
SPEND ETERNITY
IN HEAVEN.

So what does it mean to believe in Jesus for your salvation? When missionary John G. Paton was translating the New Testament for the residents of the New Hebrides islands, he sought a word that would convey "belief" or "faith." One day, he lifted his feet off the ground, leaned back in his chair, and asked one of the islanders to describe what he was doing. The man said in his native language, "You are leaning wholly on the chair." Instantly, Paton knew he had found the word he was looking for.[1]

That is what it means to believe in Jesus. It means you put your whole weight upon Him. It means you trust in Jesus alone for your salvation. You depend on that and nothing else—not your works, not your baptism, not your church membership. You trust in Jesus alone.

What's the difference between believing something intellectually and "putting your whole weight on" something?

What would it look like to put your whole weight on God every day?

God, I want to put my whole weight on You—for my salvation and for living every day. Help me to depend upon You for all my needs.

DAY 52

Our Need and God's Provision

For God so loved the world, that He gave His only begotten Son, that whoever believes in Him shall not perish, but have eternal life.

—John 3:16

In John 3, Jesus explained to Nicodemus, a respected Jewish leader, what it meant to be "born again." Jesus used this illustration in verses 14–15: "As Moses lifted up the serpent in the wilderness, even so must the Son of Man be lifted up; so that whoever believes will in Him have eternal life."

In Numbers 21, the children of Israel were disobedient to God, so God disciplined them by sending fiery serpents. The people begged for relief, and Moses went to God on their behalf. God told Moses to make a serpent out of bronze, put it on a pole, and lift that pole high. Those who were bitten could look at that bronze serpent and be healed instantly. This was an illustration of a far greater truth that one day the Son of God would come to heal us of our spiritual sickness. God offers us Christ as the provision for our salvation, but in order to be saved we have to exercise faith.

You and I have a desperate need. God has abundant provision to meet that need.

You and I have a desperate need. God has abundant provision to meet that need. And our faith is what bridges the gap between God's provision and our need. We have to exercise faith in order to live. It's not the quantity of our faith that matters; it's the object of our faith that matters. Only when we realize we cannot heal ourselves and look at the Savior will we live for all eternity. Jesus added in John 3:16, "For God so loved the world, that He gave His only begotten Son, that whoever believes in Him shall not perish, but have eternal life."

How would you explain our desperate need for salvation to someone who doesn't think they need God?

Lord, thank You for providing abundantly to meet my desperate need for a Savior. Help me to hold up Jesus Christ to those around me who need salvation.

DAY 53

A Variety of Lies

See to it that no one takes you captive through philoso-
phy and empty deception, according to the tradition
of men, according to the elementary principles of the
world, rather than according to Christ.
—Colossians 2:8

The blockbuster movie *Titanic* told the story of one of
the worst disasters of the twentieth century. However, the
screenwriters missed perhaps one of the most dramatic
scenes of that story. After news broke of the *Titanic's* sink-
ing, people began to gather in front of the offices of the
White Star Line in Southampton, England, the port city
where the *Titanic* had embarked on her maiden voyage.
Most of the crew were from Southampton, so their loved
ones were desperate for news. They waited. A few days after
the wreck, blackboards were nailed up to hold the names
of those known to be saved—but there were no names yet.

AT THE MOMENT OF DEATH, THERE ARE ONLY TWO CATEGORIES THAT MATTER: SAVED AND LOST.

So the vigil continued. It would be two more days until a clerk came out with little strips of paper and pasted them onto the blackboards, and people crowded around to see who had been saved.[1]

Interestingly, just a few days earlier, the twenty-two hundred people on that ship were having all kinds of different experiences. Some were enjoying first-class service; others were in second class or third class; many from Southampton were serving as stewards or toiling in the engine rooms. But after the ship sank, there were only two categories: saved and lost.

In our world today, people also have a diversity of experiences and come from a variety of backgrounds. But at the moment of death there are only two categories that matter: saved and lost. Those who are "lost"—people who will spend eternity in hell—have embraced a variety of lies but have all rejected the same truth: that Jesus Christ is the only means by which a person may be saved.

What are some common lies people embrace?

Which of those lies have eternal consequences?

God, may I not put so much stock in my status, possessions, and accomplishments in this life and instead prioritize the next life. Help me to share the truth about eternity with those who have embraced lies.

DAY 54

You Don't Go to Heaven in a Group

Repent, and each of you be baptized in the name of Jesus Christ for the forgiveness of your sins.

—*Acts 2:38*

When I was young, the amusement park Six Flags Over Texas opened in Arlington, Texas. In those early years, people would assemble in the plaza outside the gate—sometimes hours before the park opened. When the park opened, everybody would rush to the entrance. But people couldn't enter en masse, or even as families. There was a turnstile, and we all had to go through it one by one to get into the park.

It's the same way when going to heaven. Nobody goes to heaven in a group. No families are welcomed into heaven as a group; no denominations are welcomed into heaven as a group. I'm often asked by the media, "Do you believe Catholics are going to heaven? Do you believe Protestants are going to heaven? Do you believe Jews are going to heaven?"

Nobody goes to heaven in a group.

I always answer the same way: "No one goes to heaven in a group. We go individually based on our relationship to Jesus Christ."

What about people around the world who have rejected their knowledge of Jesus Christ and chosen another path? Is there salvation for them? Jesus answered that question not only by His words but also by His example. Think about this: If there's some way to be saved other than through Jesus Christ, why did Jesus go through that horrific physical and spiritual suffering on the cross? He did so because there's no other way to heaven—not attending a certain church, not being part of a Christian family, not even getting baptized. Jesus Christ is the only way to heaven.

Do you know anybody who believes they will go to heaven because of what they do or who they're related to?

What will you do to help them learn the truth?

Lord, I pray for those I know who are under misconceptions about how to go to heaven. Open their hearts to hear and accept the gospel.

DAY 55

How the New Testament Answers the Exclusivity Question

All Scripture is inspired by God.
—2 Timothy 3:16

Jesus said He is the only way to heaven. But what does the rest of the New Testament say about this subject? First, we need to understand that the rest of the New Testament is just as inspired as the words of Jesus Christ.

Several years ago, I appeared on Bill Maher's *Real Time* program on HBO. He asked me how I could reconcile my belief in capital punishment with Jesus's teaching to turn the other cheek. I said, "Jesus was talking about personal offenses, but in Romans 13 the Bible says God has given government the power of the sword to avenge evildoers."

THE REST OF THE NEW TESTAMENT IS JUST AS INSPIRED AS THE WORDS OF JESUS CHRIST.

Bill interrupted, "But Paul wrote that, not Jesus."

I said, "Yes, but Paul's words in the Bible were just as inspired as Jesus's words." Bill let out this falsetto "Whaaaaaat?" and the audience howled with laughter. I continued, "That's right, Bill. Remember both Jesus's and Paul's words are all found in the same book."[1]

In 2 Timothy 3:16, Paul wrote, "All Scripture is inspired by God." Paul wasn't just talking about the Old Testament here—at this point, most of the New Testament had already been written. In 1 Timothy 5:18, Paul equated the authority of Deuteronomy with the authority of Luke's Gospel. And the apostle Peter equated Paul's words with "the rest of the Scriptures" in 2 Peter 3:16. So when we look at this issue of whether there's only one way to heaven, we consider not only what Jesus said but also what the other New Testament writers said. And we come to the conclusion that all the New Testament writers believed not all roads lead to heaven.

What does it mean that the Bible is "inspired by God"?

Why do you think some people place more importance on the words of Jesus than on the rest of Scripture? What can you say to counter that argument?

Lord, thank You for providing an authoritative, inerrant resource for us to learn more about You. Teach me to treasure every word of Your Scripture.

DAY 56

The Example of the Apostle Peter

Let all the house of Israel know for certain that God has made Him both Lord and Christ—this Jesus whom you crucified.

—Acts 2:36

What did the apostle Peter teach about the exclusivity of Jesus Christ? Acts 2 recounts the feast of Pentecost. Jews had traveled from all over to Jerusalem to celebrate—the same Jews who had been in Jerusalem for Passover when Jesus was crucified. Peter stood on the steps of the temple and said to them, "Jesus the Nazarene . . . you nailed to a cross by the hands of godless men and put Him to death. But God raised Him up again. . . . Let all the house of Israel know for certain that God has made Him both Lord and Christ—this Jesus whom you crucified" (vv. 22–24, 36). Talk about courageous—Peter looked at the murderers of Jesus and said, "He was the Christ; you nailed Him to the cross."

Peter's words could have incited a riot. But notice how the people responded: "They were pierced to the heart, and said to Peter and the rest of the apostles, 'Brethren, what shall we do?'" (v. 37).

Peter could have said, "What? You're Jews. You keep the feasts and offer the sacrifices. You don't need to do any-

Judaism is not enough. You need to personally trust in Christ as your Savior.

thing." Look at what he said instead: "Repent, and each of you be baptized in the name of Jesus Christ for the forgiveness of your sins" (v. 38). I think it's significant that the first sermon preached after the resurrection of Jesus Christ was preached by a Jew, the apostle Peter, to a group of Jews. And the message of the first sermon was this: Judaism is not enough. You need to personally trust in Christ as your Savior.

If you were face-to-face with the people who crucified Jesus, how do you think you would respond?

What do you learn from Peter's sermon?

God, Your Word makes it clear that even Your chosen people must believe in Jesus for their salvation. Help me to be like Peter, sharing the gospel with boldness and conviction.

DAY 57

No Other Name

There is salvation in no one else; for there is no other name under heaven that has been given among men by which we must be saved.

—Acts 4:12

A few weeks after the crucifixion, Acts 2 shows us the apostle Peter standing on the southern steps of the temple in Jerusalem, preaching to the very same people who a few weeks earlier had cried, "Crucify Him!" And he told these Jews that the only way to be saved from their sins was to believe in Jesus Christ.

Two chapters later, in Acts 4, Peter and the apostles were teaching in the name of Jesus. Verse 4 says five thousand Jews had converted to Christianity. It was spreading like wildfire, and the Jewish authorities were panicked. They said, "We've got to put a stop to this." So they hauled in Peter and the apostles and demanded, in essence, "We want to know in what name you are teaching and healing" (v. 7).

Thank goodness Peter wasn't infected with a case of political correctness like so many Christians today. He didn't reason to himself, *I don't want to offend these Jewish leaders, so I won't use the name of Jesus; I'll just say the name of God.* No, he didn't do that. He said, "Let it be known to all of you and to all the people of Israel, that by the name of Jesus Christ the Nazarene, whom you crucified, whom God raised from the dead—by this name this man stands here before you in good health. . . . And there is salvation in no one else; for there is no other name under heaven that has been given among men by which we must be saved" (vv. 10, 12). Peter taught that salvation is only through Jesus Christ.

> *Peter taught that salvation is only through Jesus Christ.*

Have you ever avoided sharing God's truth in order not to offend somebody? What happened?

What's the difference between sharing an offensive truth and sharing the truth offensively?

Lord, give me the desire to please You rather than to please others. Help me share Your message of salvation, even when that message may offend people.

141

DAY 58

The Right Person with the Right Name

At the name of Jesus every knee will bow, of those who are in heaven and on earth and under the earth, and . . . every tongue will confess that Jesus Christ is Lord.

—Philippians 2:10–11

Today, it's popular for inclusivists to say that people can be saved by Jesus without knowing the name of Jesus. Inclusivists say, "People are worshiping the same God; they just call Him a different name."

Let me show you how ridiculous that is. Imagine you are working on a project with a coworker. He says, "Can you get a signature from the boss?" You reply, "Sure thing!"

The next day, you come in with a signed document. Your coworker looks at the signature and furrows his brow. "You were supposed to get a signature from the boss," he says.

IT DOESN'T
MATTER WHO
YOU THINK YOU
ARE TRUSTING
FOR SALVATION;
IT HAS TO BE
THE RIGHT
PERSON WITH
THE RIGHT NAME.

"Whose signature is this?" You say, "Cindy, of course." "But the boss is Janet." You reply, "Well, the boss I know is Cindy. Surely the name doesn't matter all that much. We got a signature from the boss, didn't we?"

But when the document goes to the legal department, they say, "Sorry, we need Janet's signature. Cindy's not the right person." It doesn't matter who you think is the boss; it has to be the right name on that document.

In the same way, it doesn't matter who you think you are trusting for salvation; it has to be the right person with the right name. Names mean something. When we talk about the name of Jesus, we're talking about the person of Jesus. It doesn't matter what language you translate that name into; it refers to the person who came to earth, died, and rose again that we might have eternal life. That's the only name by which we are saved.

When you hear the name Jesus, what comes to your mind?

How can you respond to somebody who believes religious people are all worshiping the same God by different names?

Lord, help me not to compromise on the issue of Your identity. Renew my confidence in the person and the name of Jesus for my salvation.

It's Not Enough to Be Devout

> *Of Him all the prophets bear witness that through His name everyone who believes in Him receives forgiveness of sins.*
>
> —*Acts 10:43*

Peter taught the exclusivity of salvation through faith in Christ alone. We see that not only in Peter's teaching but also in his ministry. Look at Acts 10:1–2: "There was a man at Caesarea named Cornelius . . . a devout man and one who feared God with all his household, and gave many alms to the Jewish people and prayed to God continually." God said that wasn't enough. So He sent Peter to Cornelius's house to share with him the only way he could be saved.

Let's imagine Cornelius invited Peter in, and Peter discovered that Cornelius was devout, prayed, and gave his

WE'RE AFRAID
OF OFFENDING
PEOPLE BY SAYING
THEIR RELIGION
ISN'T ENOUGH.

money to the poor. Peter could have said, "Cornelius, everything is just right with you. Let's just sing 'Kumbaya,' and I'll go on my way." That's what most of us would have done. We're afraid of offending people by saying their religion isn't enough. Not Peter. He told Cornelius about Jesus, and then he closed with these words: "He ordered us to preach to the people, and solemnly to testify that this is the One who has been appointed by God as Judge of the living and the dead. Of Him all the prophets bear witness that through His name everyone who believes in Him receives forgiveness of sins" (vv. 42–43). Luke wrote that Cornelius believed what he heard and trusted in Christ.

If Cornelius was already going to heaven because of his sincere belief in God, then Peter wasted a trip to Caesarea. Peter knew Cornelius needed something else, and that something else was the gospel of Jesus Christ.

How do we know sincere belief in God isn't enough to go to heaven?

What do you learn from Peter's approach to sharing the gospel with Cornelius?

God, may I be willing, as Peter was, to go out of my way to share the gospel with those who need to hear it.

DAY 60

The World's Most Famous Jew Who Found Jesus

> *If anyone else has a mind to put confidence in the flesh,*
> *I far more: circumcised the eighth day, of the nation of*
> *Israel, of the tribe of Benjamin, a Hebrew of Hebrews;*
> *as to the Law, a Pharisee.*
>
> *—Philippians 3:4–5*

One of the "gotcha" questions the media loves to ask pastors is this: "Do you believe that a sincere Jew who follows his or her religion but never accepts Christ will spend eternity in hell?" I've seen pastors stutter and stammer when trying to answer that question. Finally, they say, "Well, we have to leave that up to God."

I have found the best way to answer that question is head-on. Yes, the sincere Jew who practices his or her faith without accepting Christ is going to hell, just as the sincere

Muslim, Hindu, Catholic, or Baptist who follows religion without ever accepting Christ will spend eternity in hell. How can I say that with confidence? Because the three most prominent Jews of the New Testament—Jesus, the apostle Peter, and the apostle Paul—all said there is no salvation apart from faith in Jesus Christ.

If religion could save anyone, it should have saved Paul.

If anyone could be saved by their religious credentials apart from Christ, it should have been the apostle Paul. In Philippians 3, Paul recounted his spiritual pedigree: "Circumcised the eighth day, of the nation of Israel, of the tribe of Benjamin, a Hebrew of Hebrews; as to the Law, a Pharisee; as to zeal, a persecutor of the church; as to the righteousness which is in the Law, found blameless" (vv. 5–6). Paul believed he was doing God's work. If religion could save anyone, it should have saved Paul. But Paul's experience demonstrates that sincerity of religion isn't enough.

What is on your spiritual résumé?

How do you think God views your spiritual pedigree?

Lord, keep me from being prideful about my own spiritual "accomplishments," instead recognizing that it's by Your grace alone that I am saved.

DAY 61

Not Ashamed of the Gospel

I am not ashamed of the gospel, for it is the power of
God for salvation to everyone who believes.
—*Romans 1:16*

Paul had an impeccable spiritual résumé. Yet he was still on the road to hell until he had a life-changing encounter. Acts 9:3–5 says, "He was approaching Damascus, and suddenly a light from heaven flashed around him; and he fell to the ground and heard a voice saying to him, 'Saul, Saul, why are you persecuting Me?' And he said, 'Who are You, Lord?' And He said, 'I am Jesus whom you are persecuting.'" That confrontation transformed Paul from being the greatest antagonist of Christianity to the greatest evangelist for the Christian faith.

Paul's own experience demonstrates that sincerity of religion isn't enough to enter heaven. We also see that in his ministry. Paul wasn't like many Christians today who say, "I personally believe that faith in Christ is the only way to be saved, but I don't want to impose that belief on other people." Not Paul. He said in Romans 1:16, "I am not ashamed of the gospel, for it is the power of God for salvation to everyone who believes."

If we're honest, I think all of us would say there are times we've demonstrated by our actions that we're ashamed of the gospel: when we refuse to speak out when somebody is attacking Christianity, when we fail to share the gospel with somebody, when we refuse to lovingly say to a sincere follower of another faith, "There is only one way to heaven." We all demonstrate that we're ashamed, in a way, of the gospel when we refuse to speak out, but not the apostle Paul. He never backed down from proclaiming there's only one way to heaven.

> *Sincerity of religion isn't enough to enter heaven.*

Can you recall a time when you were ashamed of the gospel? What happened?

If you could relive that experience, what would you do differently?

Lord, forgive me for those times I have been ashamed of the gospel. Help me to be more like Paul in proclaiming the truth about salvation.

151

DAY 62

The Ministry of the Apostle Paul

I have been in labor and hardship, through many sleepless nights, in hunger and thirst, often without food, in cold and exposure.

—2 Corinthians 11:27

The apostle Paul didn't back down from preaching the exclusivity of Christ for salvation. In 2 Corinthians 11:24–27, Paul gave this testimony about what he endured for preaching the gospel: "Five times I received from the Jews thirty-nine lashes. Three times I was beaten with rods, once I was stoned, three times I was shipwrecked, a night and a day I have spent in the deep. I have been on frequent journeys, in dangers from rivers, dangers from robbers, dangers from my countrymen, dangers from the Gentiles, dangers in the city, dangers in the wilderness, dangers on the sea, dangers

IF EVERYBODY IS
GOING TO HEAVEN
REGARDLESS
OF WHAT THEY
BELIEVE, WHY
DID PAUL RISK
HIS OWN LIFE
TO PREACH THE
GOSPEL?

among false brethren; I have been in labor and hardship, through many sleepless nights, in hunger and thirst, often without food, in cold and exposure."

Now, here is the simple question: If everybody is going to heaven regardless of what they believe, why did Paul risk his own life to preach the gospel? Why did he go through all these hardships? Why was he ultimately willing to be killed for proclaiming the way to heaven if everybody is going to heaven anyway?

Paul was willing to go through all this not because he believed Jesus was just another way to heaven but because he believed faith in Christ was the only way to be saved. That's why he said in Romans 1:16, "I am not ashamed of the gospel, for it is the power of God for salvation to everyone who believes."

Do you think Paul would have been willing to endure everything he did if there were another way to heaven?

How strong is your belief in the exclusivity of Christ for salvation?

God, I pray You will keep me safe from persecution like the apostle Paul experienced. But I also pray You will strengthen my faith to endure any hardship.

DAY 63

The Divine Rescue Plan

All of us like sheep have gone astray, each of us has turned to his own way.

—Isaiah 53:6

Thirteen times in the book of Romans, Paul used the word *salvation* or *save*. We use that term *salvation* so often in the church that we sometimes forget what it really means. Salvation means "rescue from danger." And in Romans 1:16, Paul linked salvation to the gospel: "I am not ashamed of the gospel, for it is the power of God for salvation to everyone who believes." That word *gospel* literally means "good news." Paul was saying, "I am not ashamed of the good news, because it's the power of God for rescuing everyone who believes."

The Academy Award–winning movie *Gravity* tells the story of two astronauts who are stranded in outer space. They are in a space capsule, drifting farther and farther away from earth and looking for a way back home. Any plan from Mission Control that would allow them to come back to earth would be good news.

The Bible says the moment we draw our first breath, we start drifting farther and farther away from God. Isaiah 53:6 says, "All of us like sheep have gone astray, each of us has turned to his own way." God could leave us to suffer the eternal results of our separation from Him, but instead, because of the great love God has for you and me, He instituted a rescue plan to bring us back home again. And that rescue plan is the gospel of Jesus Christ. That's why Paul said, in essence, "I don't hesitate to preach the gospel to everyone because it's the only way for a person to be rescued."

> *The moment we draw our first breath, we start drifting farther and farther away from God.*

Have you ever rescued somebody from a difficult or uncomfortable situation? What motivated you to come to their aid?

What motivation do you have to share the gospel with people?

Lord, thank You for rescuing me from the eternal consequences of sin. May I never lose sight of that good news! Help me to never back down in sharing Your rescue plan with others.

The Teaching of the Apostle Paul

For in [the gospel] the righteousness of God is revealed from faith to faith.

—Romans 1:17

The apostle Paul didn't believe in the inclusivist view of salvation that says, "Because Christ died for the sins of the world, everyone is going to heaven whether they personally believe or not." Some Christians believe the death of Christ resulted in salvation for everybody whether or not they believe in Christ or even know the name of Christ.

That's not what Paul said. Notice in Romans 1:16 he didn't say the gospel "is the power of God for salvation to everyone." No, he said the gospel "is the power of God for salvation to everyone *who believes.*" Paul believed faith was necessary to receive the rescue, the salvation, that God offers.

Just as a safety net below a burning building can only rescue somebody who will jump into it, and a life preserver in the water can only rescue somebody who will grab hold of it, so the gospel only saves those who believe in it. In Romans 1:17, Paul emphasized again the importance of faith: "For in [the gospel] the righteousness of God is revealed from faith to faith; as it is written, 'But the righteous man shall live by faith.'" Faith is what connects our need with God's provision to meet our need.

The gospel only saves those who believe in it.

We are not saved by faith; we are saved through faith. Faith is the connection between our need and God's provision. We have a need—salvation. God has a provision—Jesus Christ. Our faith is what connects God's provision with our need.

Have you ever taken a leap of faith to grab hold of an opportunity?

Have you ever *not* taken an opportunity and later regretted it? If so, how might your life be different if you had taken that leap of faith?

Lord, thank You for enabling me to take the most important leap of faith. May I help other people understand the necessity of grabbing hold of Your provision for salvation.

DAY 65

The Importance of Faith

Now apart from the Law the righteousness of God has been manifested, being witnessed by the Law and the Prophets, even the righteousness of God through faith in Jesus Christ for all those who believe.
                                                              —Romans 3:21–22

Every day we're required to exercise faith in some aspect of our lives, even if we don't realize it. My friend John Bisagno observed, "Faith is the heart of life. You go to a doctor whose name you cannot pronounce. He gives you a prescription you cannot read. You take it to a pharmacist you have never seen. He gives you medicine you do not understand and yet you take it. All in trusting, sincere *faith*!"[1]

Faith is important for this life, but it's even more important for the next life. Over and over again, Paul talked about faith connecting our need to God's provision. In Romans 3:21–26, Paul repeatedly talked about faith in relationship to salvation: "Now apart from the Law the righteousness of God has been manifested, being witnessed by the Law and the Prophets, even the righteousness of God through faith in Jesus Christ for all those who believe; for there is no distinction; for all have sinned and fall short of the glory of God, being justified as a gift by His grace through the redemption which is in Christ Jesus; whom God displayed publicly as a propitiation in His blood through faith . . . that He would be just and the justifier of the one who has faith in Jesus."

Faith is important for this life, but it's even more important for the next life.

Paul was clear we are not saved *by* faith; we are saved *through* faith. Faith is the connection between God's offer and our acceptance of it.

What are some ways you exercise faith in your day-to-day life?

How is placing your faith in Jesus different from these everyday examples of faith? How is it similar?

Lord, Your Word says faith the size of a mustard seed is enough to move mountains. Thank You for saving me through faith and helping my faith in You continue to grow.

DAY 66

An Illustration of Faith

For by grace you have been saved through faith.
—Ephesians 2:8

Paul was clear that we're not saved *by* faith; we are saved *through* faith. Let me give you an illustration to help you understand and explain this important truth.

You probably have, as I do, a television cable in your home somewhere. One end of it is attached to your television receiver and the other end is attached to a cable box. The cable simply connects your receiver to a transmitter. Now, imagine I come home one night from work, and I sit down in my favorite chair, and I see this piece of cable just sitting on my ottoman. I stare at it, and I think, *Where's my television program?* I can look at my television cable all night long, and it's not going to produce a television picture, is it? No, it has to be connected to something. It has to be connected to a transmitter, and it also has to be connected to a receiver—my television set—for me to see a picture.

It's the same way with salvation. Think of faith as that television cable. It's connected to the transmitter, the cross of Jesus Christ that transmits salvation into my life. Without this cable, there's no connection between the cross and me. This is the connection point. That's why Paul said in Ephesians 2:8, "For by grace"—God's work on the cross that I had nothing to do with—"you have been saved through faith." Does that make sense? Faith is the connection between God's offer of salvation and my acceptance.

Faith is the connection between God's offer of salvation and my acceptance.

What's the difference between being saved *by* faith and being saved *through* faith?

How would you explain saving faith to an unbeliever?

God, I want to be able to put into words what You have done in my life through faith. Please help me through Your Holy Spirit to tell people about my faith.

DAY 67

The Object of Our Faith

To the one who does not work, but believes in Him who justifies the ungodly, his faith is credited as righteousness.
—*Romans 4:5*

Yesterday I compared faith to your television cable: through faith, salvation is transmitted from the cross of Jesus Christ into your life, just like your television cable transmits a picture from your cable box to your television screen.

But now let's say your television cable is attached to your toaster instead of the cable box. Now, I don't care how long the cable is or how reliable the cable is—you aren't going to be watching any television because your toaster is completely incapable of transmitting a picture.

It's the same way with salvation. It doesn't matter how much faith I have; if I attach the other end of the cable to Hinduism, to Islam, to Buddhism, to Judaism—or even worse, if I just connect it to myself and say, "I'm going to transmit salvation through my good works"—then there is no salvation. Our faith is only as reliable as the object of our faith.

In Romans 4:5, Paul said, "To the one who does not work, but believes in Him who justifies the ungodly, his faith is credited as righteousness."

We are not saved by faith; we are saved through faith in Jesus Christ.

The moment I come to the point when I realize I can't save myself, I refuse to work for my salvation, and I believe instead in the one who declares me not guilty—Jesus Christ—God takes my faith, no matter how small it is, and He counts it as righteousness. We are not saved by faith; we are saved through faith in Jesus Christ.

Have you ever placed your faith in someone or something that failed you? What was the result?

How can you have confidence you've placed your faith in the right person for salvation?

Heavenly Father, I'm trusting in what Jesus did on the cross—not in anyone or anything else—for my salvation. Renew my confidence in Your Son and what He has done for me.

DAY 68

Beyond the Apostle Paul

He became to all those who obey Him the source of
eternal salvation, being designated by God as a high
priest according to the order of Melchizedek.
                                    —Hebrews 5:9–10

The apostle Paul, the apostle Peter, and Jesus Himself taught there's only one way to be saved. Different religions are not simply different paths up the same mountain of truth that leads to God. Today I want to look at what the writer of the book of Hebrews had to say about the exclusivity of Christ for salvation.

We don't know who wrote Hebrews, but we know this letter was written to Jewish people who had recently converted to Christianity. They had placed their faith in Jesus Christ, but because of pressure from family and friends, they were thinking about giving up their Christian beliefs and going back to Judaism. This book was written as a

JESUS CHRIST OFFERED THE SUPERIOR SACRIFICE THAT OBTAINED ETERNAL REDEMPTION.

Beyond the Apostle Paul

warning to them. The writer was saying, "Why would you give up Christianity to go back to an inferior belief system?" He showed that Christianity was superior to Judaism.

What made Christianity superior? First, Christianity had a superior priest—Jesus Christ. Judaism had human priests who sinned and had to make sacrifices for their own sin, but Jesus was the perfect high priest. Second, Christianity offered a superior sacrifice. Judaism offered the blood of animals, but Jesus Christ offered the sacrifice of Himself. Third, Christianity offered a superior salvation. In Judaism, the sacrifices had to be offered over and over again, but Jesus Christ offered the superior sacrifice that obtained eternal redemption.

Why would you give up something superior for an inferior religion? The writer of Hebrews emphasized that Christianity isn't only a better way; it's the only way to be saved.

In what ways is Christianity superior to other belief systems?

How might you explain this to somebody who sincerely follows a different religion?

Lord, thank You for providing a superior High Priest who offered a superior sacrifice for my sins. Help me to lovingly explain the superiority of Christ to those who follow other beliefs.

DAY 69

The Danger of Drifting

For this reason we must pay much closer attention to what we have heard, so that we do not drift away from it.

—Hebrews 2:1

Today the writer of Hebrews would be called a bigot for suggesting that Christianity was superior to any religion, especially Judaism. But over and over again, the writer warned that a dire future awaits those who abandon Christianity for any other belief system. Look at his warning in Hebrews 2:1: "For this reason we must pay much closer attention to what we have heard, so that we do not drift away from it."

The writer used two nautical terms in this verse to make his point. "Pay closer attention" is a translation of a Greek word that refers to tying up a boat to its mooring so it will stay in place. He was saying, "If you don't want to keep drifting farther away from God and spend eternity separated from Him, you must tie up to the gospel of Jesus Christ."

What happens if you don't? The second phrase, "so that we do not drift away," refers to a ship that, through the inattention of its sailors, accidentally drifts by the harbor. The writer was saying you and I need to pay close attention to the gospel lest we neglect to take advantage of it and drift past it.

If you reject the gospel, or if you simply neglect it, exactly what is your plan to get to heaven one day?

If you reject the gospel, or if you simply neglect it, exactly what is your plan to get to heaven one day? The consistent teaching of Paul, Peter, the writer of Hebrews, and most importantly Jesus Christ was this: there is no other harbor that leads to safety except through faith in Jesus Christ.

Have you ever missed an important opportunity? What did you lose out on as a result?

What did you learn from that experience?

God, I'm grateful to have grabbed hold of the gospel, and I don't want other people to miss their opportunity. Please use me to help others find the safe harbor of salvation.

DAY 70

It's Not Fair!

Always [be] ready to make a defense to everyone who
asks you to give an account for the hope that is in you.

—1 Peter 3:15

Every parent who has ever disciplined a child is familiar
with these three words: "It's not fair!" Even when the evidence is too overwhelming to deny their guilt, children will
object that the punishment is far too severe for the crime
committed.

It should be no surprise that "It's not fair!" is also the
primary objection people have to the foundational belief
that the only way to escape hell is through faith in Jesus
Christ. Some people, like a child caught with a hand in the
cookie jar, want to deny their guilt. Other people admit, "I
may be slightly flawed, but hell is far too severe a punishment for not believing the right things about Jesus." And
when you talk about those who have never heard about

WHAT ABOUT ALL THE PEOPLE IN THE WORLD WHO HAVE NEVER HEARD ABOUT JESUS? IT IS VITAL THAT CHRISTIANS ARE ABLE TO ANSWER THIS QUESTION.

Jesus, the "It's not fair!" protest resounds much more loudly: "Are you saying the only way a person can go to heaven is by trusting in Jesus, and therefore if they have not heard about Jesus, they're going to be confined to an eternity in hell? It's not fair!"

So what about all the people in the world who have never heard about Jesus? It is vital that Christians are able to answer this question. The Bible says we ought to be ready to give an answer to everyone who asks us to explain the hope that is within us (1 Pet. 3:15).

If somebody were to ask you, "What about those who have never heard about Jesus?" would you know how to answer in a way that person could understand? We will examine several biblical truths that answer the question clearly.

Have you ever felt it's not fair for unbelievers to go to hell? Why did you feel this way?

How would you answer somebody who expresses this objection?

Lord, I want to be ready to answer the questions and objections people have about Your plan of salvation. Help me make it a priority to prepare my heart and mind for these encounters.

DAY 71

Everyone Is Guilty before God

There is none righteous, not even one.
—Romans 3:10

What about those who have never heard about Jesus? Do they end up in hell? The first understanding we need in order to answer this question is this: everyone is guilty before God.

To the secularist who believes that people are basically good, the idea of anybody going to hell is preposterous. "Maybe mass murderers and child rapists deserve to go to hell," they say, "but most people don't." That isn't the starting place of the gospel. The gospel begins by saying everyone is guilty before God. There is no good news of salvation unless we understand the bad news, and that's our guilt before God.

Paul spent the first three chapters of the book of Romans declaring humanity's guilt before God. He said the

Jew is guilty. The Gentile is guilty. The religious person is guilty. The pagan is guilty. Then he closed in Romans 3:9–10 with these words: "What then? Are we better than they? Not at all; for we have already charged that both Jews and Greeks are all under sin; as it is written, 'There is none righteous, not even one.'" No one is in a right standing before God.

There is no good news of salvation unless we understand the bad news.

How can that be true? In Romans 5:12, Paul said, "Through one man [Adam] sin entered into the world, and death through sin, and so death spread to all men, because all sinned." When Adam sinned, his sin virus was passed on to every man, woman, boy, and girl who has ever lived. And the fact that people die is proof. Every one of us has inherited the sin virus.

Do you think the average person believes he or she is guilty?

How would you convince somebody who believes people are basically good that everyone is guilty before God?

Lord, You are holy, and I am not. Thank You for helping me recognize my guilt before You, and thank You for forgiving my sins. May the people around me also recognize their need for forgiveness.

DAY 72

The Unfairness of Salvation

For if by the transgression of the one [Adam], death reigned through the one, much more those who receive the abundance of grace and of the gift of righteousness will reign in life through the One, Jesus Christ.

—Romans 5:17

Everybody who has ever lived has inherited the sin virus from Adam. What did we inherit? We inherited not only Adam's inclination to sin but also Adam's guilt. A lot of people have trouble with that. They say, "Wait a minute. Are you saying we're held responsible for what Adam did?" Absolutely. Then you hear the protest: "It's not fair that I would be held guilty for what another person did!" Even though every hour of every day, you and I confirm Adam's

WE INHERITED
NOT ONLY ADAM'S
INCLINATION TO
SIN BUT ALSO
ADAM'S GUILT.

choice when we sin against God, don't we? But people say, "It's not fair that I would be held guilty for what Adam did."

Paul anticipated that argument. He said in Romans 5:17, "For if by the transgression of the one [Adam], death reigned through the one, much more those who receive the abundance of grace and of the gift of righteousness will reign in life through the One, Jesus Christ." Paul was saying, "Yes, we are all held guilty because of Adam's sin, but here's something even more unfair—that you and I can be declared righteous before God by what one person, Jesus Christ, did for us. That is unfair too!"

Aren't you glad God is unfair in that He credits us with the righteousness of Jesus Christ, even though we don't deserve it? That is the essence of the gospel message.

Have you ever been blamed for what somebody else did wrong? Have you received something good that you didn't deserve?

How do those experiences affect your perspective on humanity's guilt and God's grace?

God, when I'm tempted to doubt Your judgment, help me to remember Your grace in crediting me with Christ's righteousness.

DAY 73

The Reality of the Wrath of God

He who does not obey the Son will not see life, but the wrath of God abides on him.

—John 3:36

Because every one of us is guilty before God, every one of us is deserving of the wrath, or the punishment, of God. Today, it's very unpopular to talk about the wrath of God. People will applaud you if you talk about the love of God or even the justice of God, but nobody wants to hear about the wrath of God. It sounds like something from the Victorian era or the Puritan era. It just doesn't seem relevant today.

Yet the wrath of God is a reality. If you do a study in a Bible concordance, you will find that the wrath or the anger of God is mentioned far more than the love of God. For example, in John 3:16, Jesus uttered what became the most popular verse of the New Testament: "For God so loved the world, that He gave His only begotten Son." But in that very same chapter, Jesus also said, "He who believes in the Son has eternal life; but he who does not obey the Son will not see life, but the wrath of God abides on him" (v. 36). Or Romans 1:18: "The wrath of God is revealed from heaven against all ungodliness and unrighteousness of men who suppress the truth in unrighteousness." Or Ephesians 5:6: "Let no one deceive you with empty words, for because of these things the wrath of God comes upon the sons of disobedience."

God's love and God's wrath are both part of His nature.

You can't strip one attribute away from God just because you don't like it. God's love and God's wrath are both part of His nature.

Is there any attribute of God you tend to ignore or deny?

How would you explain to someone that God is both loving and wrathful?

Lord, I know it's unpopular and even uncomfortable to talk about Your wrath, but Your Word says it is part of Your nature. Let me not shy away from who You are as I tell others about You.

DAY 74

The Meaning of the Wrath of God

The wrath of God is revealed from heaven against all ungodliness and unrighteousness of men.
                                                    —*Romans 1:18*

What do we mean when we talk about the wrath of God? There are two Greek words that are translated "anger" or "wrath" in the Bible. The first is *thumos*. This word refers to an explosive anger that wells up quickly and also subsides quickly. It's that emotion you feel when somebody cuts you off on the highway or says something that rubs you the wrong way. You get furious, but hopefully you get over it.

The second Greek word translated "anger" or "wrath" is *orge*. This is the term Paul used in Romans to describe God's wrath. Leon Morris defined *orge* as "a strong and settled opposition to all that is evil arising out of God's own

The Meaning of the Wrath of God

nature."[1] When we sin, God doesn't lose His temper, pour out His anger, and then get over it. Instead, God's wrath is His building opposition to everything unholy. Think of God's wrath as the water that builds up behind a dam and will eventually break through that dam. The anger of God is building and building, and one day it will be unleashed upon ungodliness.

> *The anger of God is building and building, and one day it will be unleashed upon ungodliness.*

Sometimes the water that's building behind the dam spills over onto the people below before the dam bursts. And it's the same thing with the wrath of God. Yes, there's a future day of God's wrath, but right now we experience the result of His holy revulsion for breaking His laws in our everyday lives.

Have you felt (or been on the receiving end of) *thumos*, that explosive anger? What happened?

How is that kind of anger different from *orge*, the wrath of God?

God, I'm grateful that I serve a holy God who is higher and better than I am. Help me to understand both Your wrath and Your mercy.

DAY 75

How We Experience God's Wrath

[If] My people who are called by My name humble themselves and pray and seek My face and turn from their wicked ways, then I will hear from heaven, will forgive their sin and will heal their land.

—*2 Chronicles 7:14*

We individually feel God's wrath when we break God's laws. Whenever we ignore God's commands, we experience natural consequences such as broken relationships, divorce, and illness. In Romans 1:18, Paul said, "The wrath of God is revealed from heaven against all ungodliness and unrighteousness of men who suppress the truth in unrighteousness."

That's not only true for us individually but true for our nation as well. No nation can reject God and be blessed by God. What's the cure for the depravity and divisiveness in our country right now? It's the same cure God gave three

No nation can reject God and be blessed by God.

thousand years ago to His people in 2 Chronicles 7:14: "[If] My people who are called by My name humble themselves and pray and seek My face and turn from their wicked ways, then I will hear from heaven, will forgive their sin and will heal their land."

The final unleashing of the wrath of God is described in Revelation 20: "I saw a great white throne and Him who sat upon it. . . . And I saw the dead, the great and the small, standing before the throne, and books were opened. . . . And if anyone's name was not found written in the book of life, he was thrown into the lake of fire" (vv. 11–12, 15).

The ultimate unleashing of God's wrath will be at that final judgment when everyone who has ever lived will be sentenced to the punishment they deserve. The only people who will be exempted are those who've trusted in Christ as Savior and have their name written in the Lamb's book of life.

In what ways have you or somebody you know experienced God's wrath in this life?

How does Revelation 20:11–15 affect your desire to share the gospel?

Heavenly Father, thank You for providing a way to avoid the ultimate unleashing of Your wrath. May I take advantage of the time we have until that day to help others escape Your wrath.

DAY 76

Natural Revelation

Since the creation of the world His invisible attributes,
His eternal power and divine nature, have been clearly
seen, being understood through what has been made,
so that they are without excuse.

—Romans 1:20

If faith in Jesus Christ is the only way to be saved, what about people who have never heard about Jesus? When people ask that question, you can assure them that everybody who has ever lived has received knowledge of God.

A college professor constructed an elaborate model of our solar system. A student saw that model and asked, "Prof, who made this?" The professor said, "No one." The student laughed and said, "No, really, who made this?" The professor repeated, "No one." Irritated, the student said, "Are you telling me this just happened?" The professor said, "If you can look at the entire universe and say, 'It just

CREATION IS A TESTIMONY OF THE POWER OF GOD.

happened,' then you should have no problem believing this model happened by itself."

The fact is, creation is a testimony of the power of God. There is information about God that everybody can have regardless of whether they ever read a Bible or hear a sermon. We call it *natural revelation*. It is from nature.

In Paul's day, the people who had never heard the gospel were the Gentiles. As non-Jews they didn't have the benefit of the Old Testament Law or the Prophets. People asked Paul, "What about the fate of the Gentiles?" In Romans 1, Paul said the Gentile is just as guilty as the Jew who rejects Jesus Christ. How could that be? Because the Gentile is the recipient of certain information about God. Paul said in Romans 1:20, "Since the creation of the world His invisible attributes, His eternal power and divine nature, have been clearly seen, being understood through what has been made, so that they are without excuse."

When you look at the world around you, what do you learn about God?

Do you think anybody, anywhere in the world, can learn about God through His creation? Why or why not?

God, Your creation is incredible! Thank You for revealing Yourself through the world around me. Help me never to take for granted the wonders of Your creation.

DAY 77

God's Eternal Power

The heavens are telling of the glory of God; and their
expanse is declaring the work of His hands.
                                        —Psalm 19:1

Paul said there's information about God that everybody can have because it's found in nature. There are two things Paul said we can know about God from simply looking at creation. Today we will look at the first: we can know God's "eternal power" (Rom. 1:20).

Did you know astronomers can view objects in the universe that are 47 billion light-years away? Now, it's difficult for us to imagine just how far away that is. So here's another way to think about the size of the universe: if you traveled at the speed of light (186,282 miles per second), it would take you 150,000 years at that speed to cross the Milky Way. And our galaxy is just one of millions of galaxies! That's mind-boggling.

How did the universe come into being? The secularist says, "It happened by chance." But chance isn't a power; it's a mathematical probability. For example, if I flip a coin, what are the chances it will land heads up? The mathematical probability is 50/50. But if it does land heads up, what made it do so? It could have been the force of my thumb, the weight of the coin, the air pressure, or dozens of other factors. But chance had nothing to do with it, because chance isn't a power; it's a mathematical calculation.

This universe wasn't created by chance.

It's the same thing with this universe. This universe wasn't created by chance. Psalm 19:1 says, "The heavens are telling of the glory of God; and their expanse is declaring the work of His hands." Nature reveals God's eternal power.

In what ways does nature reflect God's power?

When you think about the scope of the universe, how does it make you feel? How does it make you feel about God?

Lord, I can't fathom the size of this incredible universe You have created. But I know it couldn't have happened by chance. By Your power all things were created!

God's Divine Nature

In the generations gone by He permitted all the nations to go their own ways; and yet He did not leave Himself without witness, in that He did good and gave you rains from heaven and fruitful seasons.

—*Acts 14:16–17*

Paul said there are two things we can know about God from natural revelation. First, nature tells us about God's "eternal power." Anybody can know just by looking at creation that there is a powerful God at work. Second, God's creation tells us about His "divine nature" (Rom. 1:20).

Now, there are some truths about God we can know only through the Bible or Jesus. We can look at the universe and never know God is holy, just, or all-knowing. But Paul said there are things we can know about God's nature from creation, and one of those things is God's kindness.

In Acts 14, Paul and Barnabas arrived in Lystra, and because they performed miracles, the people mistakenly thought they were gods. Paul quickly told them, "We're not gods. We're here to point you to the true God." In Acts 14:15–17, he said, "Men, why are you doing these things? We are also men of the same nature as you, and preach the gospel to you that you should turn from these vain things to a living God, who made the heaven and the earth and the sea and all that is in them. In the generations gone by He permitted all the nations to go their own ways; and yet He did

> *There are things we can know about God's nature from creation, and one of those things is God's kindness.*

not leave Himself without witness, in that He did good and gave you rains from heaven and fruitful seasons, satisfying your hearts with food and gladness."

Paul was saying, "The fact that God sends you rain to produce the crops you need tells you that God is kind." Nature reveals God's kindness, part of His divine nature.

In what ways does nature reflect God's kindness?

How do you think the world around you would be different if God were unkind?

Lord, thank You for showing us Your kindness in the ways that You care for Your creation, including me.

DAY 79

The Kindness of God

Do you think lightly of the riches of His kindness and tolerance and patience, not knowing that the kindness of God leads you to repentance?

—Romans 2:4

We can know from looking at God's creation that He is a kind God. You know, we often hear people say, "If God is good, why does He allow bad things to happen? Why does He allow floods and earthquakes and famines?" But the focus of those questions is all wrong because those bad things are usually the exception rather than the rule. Most of the time the rains do come on schedule. Most of the time the tectonic plates don't shift and cause earthquakes. So the real question is not "Why do bad things happen to good people?" but "Why do good things happen to bad people?"

God sends good things to bad people all the time. He shows kindness to them in spite of their disregard for Him.

Why? Paul said in Romans 2:4, "Do you think lightly of the riches of His kindness and tolerance and patience, not knowing that the kindness of God leads you to repentance?" God sends good things into the lives of unbelievers to cause them to turn their hearts toward Him.

Maybe you have been living far away from God. And you have thought, *If things are so wrong between me and God, why is everything in my life going so right? Good things are happening to me, not bad things.* It is because God loves you. He's trying to win you back to Himself through His kindness.

God sends good things to bad people all the time.

That's what Paul was saying: everybody is able to look at creation and know we serve a kind God.

If somebody asked, "Why does God allow bad things to happen?" how would you respond?

How does thinking of the bad things as the exception, not the rule, change your view of God's character?

God, sometimes it feels like the bad things in this world outnumber the good things. Help me to see Your kindness in Your everyday provision, even when I don't deserve it.

DAY 80

Rejecting God's Revelation

*Even though they knew God, they did not honor Him
as God or give thanks, but they became futile in their
speculations, and their foolish heart was darkened.*

—Romans 1:21

In Romans 1, Paul described the knowledge about God that
is available through nature. But most people have rejected
that knowledge of God. Romans 1:21 says, "Even though
they knew God, they did not honor Him as God or give
thanks, but they became futile in their speculations, and
their foolish heart was darkened."

Secularists say they can't find any scientific evidence of
God, and that's why they've rejected Him. But the opposite
is true. The people who reject God haven't objectively ex-
amined the evidence; they started with the presupposition
that there is no God, and they've looked for evidence to
confirm that presupposition.

THE UNBELIEVER
HAS RECEIVED
A REVELATION
ABOUT THE TRUE
GOD BUT HAS
REJECTED THAT
REVELATION.

Richard Lewontin, the late Harvard biologist and atheist, conceded this point in the *New York Review of Books*. He wrote, "We take the side of science [against the supernatural] . . . because we have a prior commitment, a commitment to materialism. It is not that the methods and institutions of science somehow compel us to accept a material explanation of the phenomenal world, but, on the contrary, that we are forced by our a priori adherence to material causes to create an apparatus of investigation and a set of concepts that produce material explanations, no matter how counterintuitive, no matter how mystifying to the uninitiated. Moreover, that materialism is absolute, for we cannot allow a Divine Foot in the door."[1]

Do you know why an atheist can't find God? It's the same reason a thief can't find a police officer—they're not looking that hard. That's what Paul was saying. The unbeliever has received a revelation about the true God but has rejected that revelation.

Have you tried to argue for God's existence with somebody who presumes there is no God? What happened?

How will you pray for people like that?

Lord, it can be frustrating to witness to people who don't want to believe in You. I pray that You would shine the light of Your truth into their hearts.

DAY 81

The Devolution
of Religion

*Professing to be wise, they became fools, and exchanged
the glory of the incorruptible God for an image in the
form of corruptible man and of birds and four-footed
animals and crawling creatures.*
—Romans 1:22–23

If you take a course in comparative religions, you'll hear
about the evolution of religion. The idea is just as humans
have evolved from amoeba to tadpole to fish to human, and
are getting more complex, so human religion is also evolv-
ing. That is, humans started out as primates and worshiped
things and other animals. That's animism. But as humans
evolved, they went from animism to polytheism, the worship of many gods. And then they evolved to monotheism,
the worship of one god.

ALL FALSE RELIGIONS ARE THE RESULT OF PEOPLE REJECTING THE KNOWLEDGE OF THE TRUE GOD AND CREATING THEIR OWN GODS.

Now, that's a great idea—except it contradicts history. The opposite is true.

Paul didn't talk about the evolution of religion but rather the devolution of religion. He wrote, "Professing to be wise, they became fools, and exchanged the glory of the incorruptible God for an image in the form of corruptible man and of birds and four-footed animals and crawling creatures" (Rom. 1:22–23).

At the beginning, people had knowledge of the one true God. Adam and Eve worshiped God in the garden of Eden. But because of sin, people began to devolve, and they exchanged the knowledge of the one true God for the worship of objects, animals, and other idols. They began creating false religions, replacing the true God with gods of their own making.

All false religions are the result of people rejecting the knowledge of the true God and creating their own gods they want to follow.

In what ways do you see people "professing to be wise" and replacing the true God with gods of their own making?

Lord, since the garden of Eden, people have exchanged a relationship with You for idols of their own making. May my relationship with You inspire others to seek out the true God.

DAY 82

The Basis of Idolatry

What profit is the idol when its maker has carved it, or an image, a teacher of falsehood? For its maker trusts in his own handiwork when he fashions speechless idols.
—Habakkuk 2:18

It isn't just followers of cults and false religions who reject the true God and create their own god. Some professing Christians do the same thing. They create a god in their own image. A. W. Tozer wrote, "Wrong ideas about God are not only the fountain from which the polluted waters of idolatry flow; they are themselves idolatrous. The idolator simply imagines things about God and acts as if they were true."[1] That's what the followers of false religions do. They create a god, imagine that god to be a certain way, and follow that god as if it were true. But so do many Christians.

Perhaps you have heard a Christian say, "I can't imagine a God who would send people to hell simply for not believing the right things about Jesus." Or, "I can't imagine a God who would condemn true, faithful love even if it was a same-sex attraction." Or, "I can't imagine a God who would tell Christians they need to stay in an unfulfilling marriage even if they're not happy."

We need to be careful not to fall into the same trap of idolatry as followers of false religions.

The operative word there is *imagine.* People assume God is the sum of their imaginings about Him, and that is the basis of idolatry. We need to be careful not to fall into the same trap of idolatry as followers of false religions. Unbelievers have replaced the revelation of the true God with the creation of their own god. Therefore Paul says they are "without excuse" (Rom. 1:20).

What do you think it means that wrong ideas about God not only lead to idolatry but are themselves idolatrous?

What are some of those wrong ideas?

God, protect me from the sin of idolatry. I pray You would draw me closer to You and away from idolatrous thoughts and ideas.

DAY 83

Natural Revelation
Is a Test

*You will seek Me and find Me when you search for Me
with all your heart.*

—Jeremiah 29:13

The Bible says salvation is only through faith in Jesus. Then what good is natural revelation? Charles Ryrie wrote, "Mankind should respond to [nature] by acknowledging that there has to be behind it all a living, powerful, intelligent, superhuman Being. If men do not make that minimal but crucial acknowledgement, but rather turn away and offer some other explanation, then God is just if He rejects them and does not offer more truth. The rejection of what is revealed in general revelation is sufficient to condemn justly. But this does not imply that the acceptance of general revelation is sufficient to effect eternal salvation."[1]

In other words, natural revelation isn't sufficient to save a person, but it is sufficient, if rejected, to condemn a person.

If somebody receives this revelation by God, they are not automatically saved, but if they reject that revelation of God, they are condemned. They are without excuse.

Anyone who wants further knowledge of God will receive it.

You see, natural revelation is a test to see if somebody really wants to know God or not. If they reject that knowledge of the true God and create their own god, then they're not really interested in knowing God. But if they're receptive to that natural revelation, then that leads to another truth we need to understand about this complex issue, and that is this: anyone who wants further knowledge of God will receive it.

Why is someone who rejects God's natural revelation "without excuse"?

What, if anything, can you do to help the people around you accept that natural revelation?

Heavenly Father, I pray for those people I know who have not come to know You. Stir up in their hearts a sincere desire to seek You.

DAY 84

God's Desire for Everyone

God our Savior . . . desires all men to be saved and to come to the knowledge of the truth.

—1 Timothy 2:3–4

Everyone has received knowledge of God, and anyone who wants further knowledge of God will receive it. You see, God's desire is to save as many people as possible, not as few people as possible. Yes, God would be just in sending everybody to hell, but that's not His desire. He wants everyone to come to a knowledge of the truth.

For example, Ezekiel 33:11 says, "'As I live!' declares the Lord GOD, 'I take no pleasure in the death of the wicked, but rather that the wicked turn from his way and live.'" In Luke 19:10, Jesus said about Himself, "The Son of Man has come to seek and to save that which was lost." Jesus's whole reason for coming to earth wasn't to condemn people but to seek them out and save them. Paul wrote in 1 Timothy

2:3–4, "God our Savior . . . desires all men to be saved and to come to the knowledge of the truth." Finally, 2 Peter 3:9 says, "The Lord is not slow about His promise, as some count slowness, but is patient toward you, not wishing for any to perish but for all to come to repentance."

God's desire is to save as many people as possible, not as few people as possible.

God desires that all people be saved. He's not saying all people *will* be saved, but His desire is that all people be saved. But the only way they can be saved is by coming to a knowledge of the truth about Jesus Christ.

How does the fact that God desires all people be saved affect your perspective of the unbelievers you encounter or read about in the news?

How does it affect your perspective of God?

God, help me to remember that You have a heart for all people, and You desire that everyone be saved. May I have that same view of the people around me.

DAY 85

The Example of Cornelius

Your prayers and alms have ascended as a memorial before God. Now dispatch some men to Joppa and send for a man named Simon, who is also called Peter.

—Acts 10:4–5

If God desires that all people be saved, then what about those who have never heard about Jesus? If somebody who has never heard about Jesus sees the evidence of God's creation through natural revelation, rejects that knowledge, and creates their own god to follow, Paul said they are without excuse. But if they receive that knowledge, if they say, "There must be someone greater than I am, and I want to know that somebody," then you can be certain God will send them further revelation of the truth of Jesus Christ.

How can I say that? How can I say these people who are beyond the reach of any missionary are going to hear the

GOD MIRACULOUSLY DIRECTED PETER TO GO TO CORNELIUS'S HOUSEHOLD TO PREACH THE GOSPEL.

gospel? Because I read the Bible. I can tell you instance after instance where God has done just that.

Earlier in this devotional, we looked at the story of Cornelius, a Roman centurion. Remember, Cornelius wanted to know the one true God. He worshiped the God of Israel, prayed to Him regularly, and gave money to the poor. Now, that should be enough by most people's standards to be saved, but not in God's economy. Cornelius needed to hear about Jesus. So what did God do? Acts 10:4–5 says an angel of God appeared to Cornelius and said, "Your prayers and alms have ascended as a memorial before God. Now dispatch some men to Joppa and send for a man named Simon, who is also called Peter." God miraculously directed Peter to go to Cornelius's household to preach the gospel, and he and his family were saved.

In what ways might God send further knowledge to those who want to know Him?

How might that look different now than in Cornelius's day?

Lord, thank You for sending further knowledge to those who want to know the true God. And may I, too, always be seeking to know You better.

The Example of the Ethiopian Eunuch

Philip ran up and heard him reading Isaiah the prophet, and said, "Do you understand what you are reading?" And he said, "Well, how could I, unless someone guides me?"

—*Acts 8:30–31*

If an unbeliever receives the knowledge of the one true God and responds by wanting to know more, you can be certain that God will send that person further revelation of the truth of Jesus Christ.

A great example of this is found in Acts 8. An Ethiopian eunuch had traveled to Jerusalem to worship the God of Israel. He was sitting in his chariot and reading the scroll of Isaiah because he wanted to know the real God. But the man's good intentions weren't enough; he needed to hear about Jesus.

WHENEVER GOD SEES SOMEBODY WHO REALLY WANTS TO KNOW HIM, HE WILL MAKE SURE THAT PERSON RECEIVES THE KNOWLEDGE OF JESUS CHRIST.

So what did God do? He miraculously sent Philip the Evangelist to him: "Philip ran up and heard him reading Isaiah the prophet, and said, 'Do you understand what you are reading?' And he said, 'Well, how could I, unless someone guides me?' And he invited Philip to come up and sit with him. . . . Then Philip opened his mouth, and beginning from this Scripture he preached Jesus to him. As they went along the road they came to some water; and the eunuch said, 'Look! Water! What prevents me from being baptized?' And Philip said, 'If you believe with all your heart, you may.' And he answered and said, 'I believe that Jesus Christ is the Son of God'" (vv. 30–31, 35–37). Isn't that a miraculous story?

Whenever God sees somebody who really wants to know Him, He will make sure that person receives the knowledge of Jesus Christ, because God is more interested in that person's salvation than you and I could ever be. Anyone who wants further knowledge of God will receive it.

Has God ever used you to deliver further knowledge of Him to someone who was seeking it?

Were you ever the recipient of such knowledge? Describe what happened.

God, help me to recognize when You are sending me to deliver further knowledge of You, and help me be better prepared to make the most of those opportunities.

211

DAY 87

The Reason God Left Us Here

You shall be My witnesses both in Jerusalem, and in all Judea and Samaria, and even to the remotest part of the earth.

—*Acts 1:8*

Every day, I hear stories of people who say things like, "I was in my car listening to the radio when I accidentally came upon your program." The older I get, the less I believe in accidents and coincidences. When God sees somebody who wants to know Him, He will send that knowledge, whether it's through an internet connection, a radio broadcast, or a conversation with a friend.

You see, God has not only ordained that people should be saved by trusting in Christ but also ordained the means by which they hear the gospel: He will send the truth through

GOD HAS NOT ONLY ORDAINED THAT PEOPLE SHOULD BE SAVED BY TRUSTING IN CHRIST BUT ALSO ORDAINED THE MEANS BY WHICH THEY HEAR THE GOSPEL.

people like you and me. That's the reason God left us here on earth.

In Matthew 28:19–20, Jesus told His disciples, in essence, "The reason I'm leaving you here and not taking you to heaven with Me is so that you will go into all the world and preach the gospel." And in Acts 1:8, He reminded them, "You shall be My witnesses both in Jerusalem, and in all Judea and Samaria, and even to the remotest part of the earth." The reason God left us here instead of taking us to heaven as soon as we were saved is to fulfill that mandate to take the gospel to everyone.

Now, none of us by ourselves can do that. None of us can singlehandedly go into all the remotest parts of the earth, or even the remotest parts of our country. That's why it's essential we band together as Christians to fulfill the mandate of Matthew 28:19–20 and the strategy of Acts 1:8.

Where have you taken the gospel?

How are you banding together with other Christians to send God's truth to the ends of the earth?

Lord, I want to respond to Your call with the same enthusiasm as the prophet Isaiah: "Here am I. Send me!" Give me a willing heart and obedient feet to take the gospel wherever You lead.

DAY 88

Are Children Who Die in Heaven?

The LORD is good to all; he has compassion on all he has made.

—*Psalm 145:9 (NIV)*

One of the most painful assignments any pastor has is trying to console parents who have lost a child. If the parents are Christians, they naturally want to know, "Will I see my child again in heaven?"

Of course, anyone with an ounce of compassion would want to assure such a parent that their child is in heaven. Maybe you have been in a similar situation, wondering what to say to a parent who has gone through that experience. Or maybe, God forbid, you personally have walked through the grief of losing a child or grandchild. But as we've discussed, the Bible teaches that only those who

I AM CONVINCED THAT INFANTS AND CHILDREN (AND BY EXTENSION, PEOPLE WITH INTELLECTUAL DISABILITIES WHO ARE "CHILDLIKE") ARE WELCOMED INTO HEAVEN WHEN THEY DIE.

have exercised faith in Jesus Christ as their Savior will be in heaven. So how does that apply to an infant or child too young to make that decision?

The fact is, there's no verse in the Bible that tells us with absolute certainty what happens to a child who dies. Yet I am convinced that infants and children (and by extension, people with intellectual disabilities who are "childlike") are welcomed into heaven when they die.

How do I come to that conclusion? That's what we're going to talk about for the next several days as we discover some truths about God's love, mercy, and justice. Although there is no single passage that clearly spells out the eternal destiny of children who die before trusting in Christ, there are five biblical principles that strongly argue that children are welcomed into heaven.

Have you tried to comfort somebody who lost a young child or grandchild? What did you say?

What do you wish you could have said?

Lord, Your love and compassion are unfailing. Help me to understand Your plan and provision for children so that I may comfort others with the truth of Your Word.

DAY 89

God's Special Love for Children

You formed my inward parts; You wove me in my mother's womb.

—Psalm 139:13

The first biblical truth that suggests children are welcomed into heaven is that God has a special love for children. God's love and concern begin before the child is born. In Psalm 139:13–16, David wrote, "You formed my inward parts; You wove me in my mother's womb. I will give thanks to You, for I am fearfully and wonderfully made; wonderful are Your works, and my soul knows it very well. My frame was not hidden from You, when I was made in secret, and skillfully wrought in the depths of the earth; Your eyes have seen my unformed substance; and in Your book were all written the days that were ordained for me, when as yet there was not one of them."

GOD'S LOVE AND CONCERN BEGIN BEFORE THE CHILD IS BORN.

In God's eyes, a fertilized egg in the mother's womb isn't some biological blob but a child whom God loves and has uniquely designed. The child in the mother's womb has a life God has ordained before that child ever draws a breath.

Because God is intimately involved in every child's life, it should be no surprise that God values children and mourns the death of children. We see that in Ezekiel 16:20–21. The Israelites had adopted the practice of sacrificing their children to the false god Moloch. God rebuked them, saying, "You took your sons and daughters whom you had borne to Me and sacrificed them to idols to be devoured. . . . You slaughtered My children."

Isn't it interesting that God referred to the children as *His* children? And God's attitude has not changed. He values children.

How do you feel knowing God loved you before you were even born?

What does the fact that God referred to the Israelites' sons and daughters as "My children" say about God's view of children?

Heavenly Father, thank You for loving me and ordaining my days even before I was born! Help me to value each and every life You have so wonderfully designed.

DAY 90

Children's Position in the Kingdom

[Jesus] said to them, "Permit the children to come to Me; do not hinder them; for the kingdom of God belongs to such as these. . . ." And He took them in His arms and began blessing them.

—Mark 10:14, 16

We see God's special love toward children in Jesus. In Matthew 18, the disciples asked Jesus who would be the greatest in the kingdom of God. So Jesus "called a child to Himself and set him before them, and said, 'Truly I say to you, unless you are converted and become like children, you will not enter the kingdom of heaven'" (vv. 2–3). Jesus randomly selected a child to make an illustration. If that little boy were going to hell if he died before reaching a certain age, then the illustration wouldn't have worked. It's nonsensical to say, "Be like this child, who is headed for hell." It doesn't work. By using that child, Jesus was saying that child would be in heaven if he died.

On another occasion, some parents brought their children to the Lord. But the disciples said, "The Lord doesn't have time for stuff like that." What was Jesus's response? "When Jesus saw this, He was indignant and said to them, 'Permit the children to come to Me; do not hinder them; for the kingdom of God belongs to such as these. . . .' And He took them in His arms and began blessing them, laying His hands on them" (Mark 10:14, 16). It doesn't make any sense that He would say that and bless these children if they were condemned to hell.

We see God's special love toward children in Jesus.

Now, this isn't evidence in and of itself of what happens to children if they die, but it's the first building block. God has a special love for children.

Why do you think God has a special love for children?

Do you think Jesus's actions and words in these verses mean all children will be in heaven? Why or why not?

God, I'm grateful to serve a God who values children, and I want to believe they're welcomed into heaven. Give me confidence in Your character.

DAY 91

God Views Children's Sin Differently

> *The person who sins will die. The son will not bear*
> *the punishment for the father's iniquity, nor will the*
> *father bear the punishment for the son's iniquity; the*
> *righteousness of the righteous will be upon himself,*
> *and the wickedness of the wicked will be upon himself.*
> —*Ezekiel 18:20*

What happens to children who die before trusting in Christ? The Bible reveals that God not only has a special love for children but also views the inherited sin of children differently than He views the willful sin of adults.

When Adam and Eve sinned because of Adam's willing disobedience, all people inherited Adam's sin. In Romans 5:12, Paul explained it this way: "Through one man [Adam] sin entered into the world, and death through sin, and so

GOD DISTINGUISHES
BETWEEN THE
INHERITED SIN
CHILDREN HAVE
RECEIVED AND
THE WILLFUL
DISOBEDIENCE
OF ADULTS.

death spread to all men, because all sinned." When Adam sinned, we inherited Adam's guilt—that is, the responsibility for his sin—and we also inherited Adam's corruption—that is, the propensity to sin against God. We've all contracted the sin virus. Paul says the proof of that is the fact that we die. Death is the evidence we have inherited Adam's sin.

Do children die? Yes. Do babies die? Yes. The fact that anyone dies is proof that he or she is guilty before God. Nevertheless, God distinguishes between the inherited sin children have received and the willful disobedience of adults. In Ezekiel 18:20, God said, "The person who sins will die. The son will not bear the punishment for the father's iniquity, nor will the father bear the punishment for the son's iniquity; the righteousness of the righteous will be upon himself, and the wickedness of the wicked will be upon himself." We are guilty for what we personally do before God.

What is the proof that we are all guilty before God?

In what ways is the disobedience of children different from that of adults?

Lord, forgive me for willfully disobeying You. Thank You for your mercy in sending Your Son to bear the punishment I deserve.

225

DAY 92

The Age of Accountability

Your little ones . . . who this day have no knowledge of good or evil, shall enter there.

—Deuteronomy 1:39

At what age are people responsible for their own sins? The phrase "age of accountability" isn't in the Bible, but there is the truth that God holds people responsible for their sin when they are able to distinguish between good and evil. Until then, God views sin differently.

A great illustration of that truth is found in Numbers 13–14. After the Israelites left Egypt, they finally made it to the promised land, and they sent twelve spies to see what obstacles they might have to overcome. Ten of the spies said, "The land is as full of blessing as God promised, but there are giants, and we'll never overtake them." Two of the spies, Joshua and Caleb, said, "Yes, there are challenges, but God will be faithful to give us the land just as He promised."

The Israelites chose to believe the majority report. God was filled with anger because of their unbelief. He said, "None of you except Joshua and Caleb are going to enter into this promised land. Instead you're going to wander in the wilderness without ever entering into My rest, and you will die because of your unbelief."

God holds people responsible for their sin when they are able to distinguish between good and evil.

But there is one group God exempted from that horrible judgment. In Deuteronomy 1:39, God said, "Your little ones . . . who this day have no knowledge of good or evil, shall enter there, and I will give it to them and they shall possess it." Even though these children had contracted the sin virus, God viewed the children's sin differently than He viewed the sins of their parents who willfully rejected God.

How would you define the "age of accountability"?

How does God view sin differently before that age?

Lord, I know You take unbelief very seriously. Help me to trust in You when I'm tempted to doubt Your promises or rebel against Your commands.

DAY 93

Children Have Not
Rejected God's Revelation

They were not able to enter because of unbelief.
—Hebrews 3:19

In the Bible, unbelief is more than simply a lack of knowledge or understanding. Unbelief is the deliberate decision to reject God's revelation.

The writer of Hebrews offered this commentary on the Israelites' sin in the wilderness. In Hebrews 3:18–19, he wrote, "To whom did [God] swear that they would not enter His rest, but to those who were disobedient? So we see that they were not able to enter because of unbelief." And he made this application in verse 12: "Take care, brethren, that there not be in any one of you an evil, unbelieving heart that falls away from the living God." The adult Israelites chose to reject the revelation God had given to them. The writer

UNBELIEF IS MORE THAN SIMPLY A LACK OF KNOWLEDGE OR UNDERSTANDING. UNBELIEF IS THE DELIBERATE DECISION TO REJECT GOD'S REVELATION.

also quoted Psalm 95: "Today if you hear His voice, do not harden your hearts as when they provoked Me, as in the day of trial in the wilderness, where your fathers tried Me by testing Me, and saw My works for forty years" (Heb. 3:7–9).

For forty years the Israelites had seen God's miraculous care for them. The adult Israelites had seen God send the plagues that changed Pharaoh's heart and caused him to let the people go. They had witnessed the miraculous parting of the Red Sea. They had experienced God's supernatural provision of manna and water. Yet they deliberately rejected the knowledge of God they had received and His promise of deliverance. Therefore, they were without excuse. But their children were too young to understand what was happening. They had not made the deliberate decision to reject what God had revealed to them.

Do you think infants and young children have willfully rejected God's revelation?

What's the difference between failing to understand the truth and willfully rejecting it?

Lord, I pray for the children in my life. May their hearts remain soft toward You, and may they come to understand Your love for them.

DAY 94

Children Have Received God's Revelation

You shall love the LORD your God with all your heart and with all your soul and with all your might. These words, which I am commanding you today, shall be on your heart. You shall teach them diligently to your sons.
—Deuteronomy 6:5–7

Paul said there is no one who is "without excuse," because everyone who has ever lived has received a revelation of God. In Romans 1:20, the apostle wrote, "Since the creation of the world His invisible attributes, His eternal power and divine nature, have been clearly seen, being understood through what has been made, so that they are without excuse." The Bible says God has revealed to everyone the fact that there is a God, and while that knowledge isn't enough to save a person, it's enough if rejected to condemn

CHILDREN HAVE
NOT REJECTED
GOD'S REVELATION;
THEY JUST HAVEN'T
ACCEPTED IT YET.

a person. Whenever anyone responds to that natural revelation of God, God will send the further information that person needs in order to know Christ as Savior.

Adults today have all received a revelation of God, and the majority have chosen to reject that revelation. Because of that they are without excuse. Contrast that to young children. They've received the revelation as well. They can look around, but they can't put it together. Therefore, God views them differently. Children have not rejected God's revelation; they just haven't accepted it yet. They're incapable of understanding it.

Now, I believe children reach the age of accountability at a much younger age than we might imagine. I think children have an understanding of right and wrong, and an understanding of God, far earlier than people would lead us to believe. And the most important job parents have is leading their children to faith in Christ and then seeing that their children grow in their faith.

What evidence do you see that young children have received God's revelation but can't understand it?

At what age do you think children begin to understand right and wrong and the idea of God?

God, give me fresh eyes to see Your hand in the world around me, and help me lead others, especially children, to understand the revelation You have given us.

233

DAY 95

A Parent's Most Important Job

Train up a child in the way he should go, even when he is old he will not depart from it.

—Proverbs 22:6

A great tragedy I see over and over again are parents who profess to be Christians prioritizing everything else in their child's life—their athletic development, their academic development, their social development—over their spiritual development. When Sunday comes around, instead of being in church, the family is out at the athletic field because their child just has to get that sports scholarship. When it's time for children's ministry activities or teen Bible study, the child isn't there because they have homework or other things to do. When the parents select a church to attend, they choose a milquetoast church that is socially acceptable but does not teach the Word of God, because they're putting their child's social development ahead of their spiritual development.

The most important task parents have is to rear their children to trust in Christ as Savior and follow Him. If you are a parent, let me encourage you to pray for your child's salvation. Make sure your child is in a Bible-believing church and taking advantage of the opportunities in that church to learn the Word of God. And finally, make sure you talk to your son or daughter about his or her need for Jesus Christ.

The most important task parents have is to rear their children to trust in Christ as Savior and follow Him.

If you don't have a child at home, maybe you have grandchildren, nieces, or nephews you can pray for and share the gospel with. Don't allow the children in your life to be guilty of rejecting God's revelation.

Is there a child in your life who has not made the decision to trust Christ as Savior? How will you pray for them?

What else can you do to support their spiritual growth?

Heavenly Father, You love the children in my life even more than I do. Grant me opportunities to share Your love with them, and give me the right words as I share Your message of salvation.

DAY 96

Salvation Is Based on God's Grace

Shall not the Judge of all the earth deal justly?
—Genesis 18:25

Why am I convinced that children who die before they accept Christ as Savior are in heaven? Because salvation is based on God's grace, not on our faith. You may say, "The Bible says only those who trust in Christ are saved. If God bends the rules for children, then why can't He bend the rules for sincere followers of other religions or those who've never heard the gospel?"

I struggled for years with this issue. All I was able to say is, "We have to depend on God to do the right thing." Abraham said in Genesis 18:25, "Shall not the Judge of all the earth deal justly?"

THE FACT THAT
A CHILD ISN'T
YET CAPABLE
OF EXERCISING
FAITH IS NO
PROBLEM
FOR GOD
WHATSOEVER.

But I've come to realize the answer to this question of how children who have never accepted Christ as Savior will be welcomed into heaven: they're saved the same way that those in the Old Testament were saved. They're saved the same way you and I are saved today. We're not saved by our faith; we're all saved by God's grace.

God's grace was demonstrated in Jesus Christ when He came and died and paid our sin debt for us. Faith is simply the way we access that grace in our lives. That's what Paul said in Ephesians 2:8–9: "By grace you have been saved through faith; and that not of yourselves, it is the gift of God; not as a result of works, so that no one may boast." The fact that a child isn't yet capable of exercising faith is no problem for God whatsoever, because that child is still saved by God's grace.

Do you think it's fair for God to "bend the rules" for children but not for other people? Why or why not?

How does the fact that we're all saved by grace affect your perspective?

God, whenever I wrestle with the implications of the exclusivity doctrine, help me to trust in Your goodness, Your justice, and Your grace.

An Illustration of Grace

For all have sinned and fall short of the glory of God, being justified as a gift by His grace through the redemption which is in Christ Jesus.
—*Romans 3:23–24*

Children who haven't personally accepted Christ as Savior are saved the same way you and I are: by God's grace. Let me illustrate that. Imagine that a woman is trapped on the third floor of a burning apartment building. She's out on the ledge. She knows she's about to die, but fortunately some firefighters are holding a net below her. She has a need, and the firefighters have the provision to meet that need. But the only way for her to access that provision is to take a leap of faith that lands her in the net. If she does so, what saved her? Was it her jumping? No, it was the net. Her faith was the way she met her need with the provision below.

Now let's change the illustration. The building is on fire, but a firefighter goes to the third floor and finds a toddler. That toddler can't comprehend what's going on. He doesn't understand how to get out, and he's incapable of jumping.

Children who haven't personally accepted Christ as Savior are saved the same way you and I are: by God's grace.

So the firefighter scoops that child up, goes to the ledge, and takes that leap into the net. What saved the toddler? The same thing that saved the woman. It was the net. The only difference is the firefighter picked up the child to allow him to access the provision below.

I think God does the same with children who are incapable of exercising faith. He scoops those children in His arms and carries them safely into heaven. Children are saved the same way we are saved—by God's grace.

How does this illustration help you understand how God saves children who haven't personally believed in Jesus?

How would you explain this to an unbeliever?

Lord, Your ways are higher than my ways and Your thoughts are higher than my thoughts. Even when I don't fully understand Your actions, help me to clearly communicate Your message.

240

The Promise of 2 Samuel 12:21–23

Can I bring him back again? I will go to him, but he will not return to me.

—2 Samuel 12:23

I believe children who die before they accept Christ as Savior are in heaven because of the promise of 2 Samuel 12:21–23. You remember the story of King David's tryst with Bathsheba, the wife of Uriah. Because of that one-night stand, Bathsheba became pregnant, and David had Uriah killed. Eventually David repented of his sin. But although God's forgiveness erased the eternal consequences of David's sin, it did not erase the temporary consequences.

After Bathsheba gave birth, the baby was sick. So David went into a time of mourning, praying, and fasting, asking God to heal his son. Surprisingly, when David was told that his son had died, he took a bath, put on new clothes, worshiped, and began to eat.

David's men were perplexed. They said in 2 Samuel 12:21, "While the child was alive, you fasted and wept; but when the child died, you arose and ate food."

David believed someday he would be reunited with his son.

David answered, "While the child was still alive, I fasted and wept; for I said, 'Who knows, the LORD may be gracious to me, that the child may live.' But now he has died; why should I fast? Can I bring him back again? I will go to him, but he will not return to me" (vv. 22–23).

David was saying, "I fasted and prayed because God might heal my child, but since He has decided not to, why should I keep doing that? I'm going to get up, put on my clothes, and get on with my life because even though my child can't come back to me, I will go to him." David believed someday he would be reunited with his son.

Why was David able to get up and get on with his life?

How does David's response to his son's death compare to your own experiences with mourning?

God, I want to be as confident as David that those who lose their children will see them again in heaven. May I find reassurance in David's faith!

242

DAY 99

Reunited in Heaven

You are good and do good; teach me Your statutes.
—Psalm 119:68

While King David's child was sick, the king refused to eat. He refused to bathe. He refused to change his clothes. But when the child died, David bathed, put on new clothes, worshiped the Lord, and began to eat. It was practically a celebration! David said to his bewildered servants, "Now he has died; why should I fast? Can I bring him back again? I will go to him, but he will not return to me" (2 Sam. 12:23).

If David's baby was on his way to hell, then David would've been saying, "My child can't come back to me, but I will go to him and be in hell forever." It doesn't make any sense to celebrate that. Some people have suggested that David was simply talking about the inevitability of death. "I will go to him" meant David would go to him in death. Does anybody want to celebrate that either? Of course not.

The only sensical interpretation of this verse is that David was celebrating the fact that his son was in the presence of God, and he rejoiced in the fact that one day he would also be in heaven to be reunited with his son and his Lord.

I think we can say with absolute certainty that God welcomes children into heaven.

Admittedly, this passage by itself doesn't make an airtight case that children are in heaven. But when you couple it with the knowledge that God is loving, just, and merciful and will do what is right, I think we can say with absolute certainty that God welcomes children into heaven.

How does the nature of God support the argument that children are welcomed into heaven?

Who are you looking forward to reuniting with in heaven?

Lord, I long for the day when I will be reunited with my loved ones in heaven. Help me to do all I can here on earth to make sure there are many people in heaven to greet me.

DAY 100

Jesus Is the Only Way

I am the way, and the truth, and the life; no one comes to the Father but through Me.

—*John 14:6*

In this devotional, we have discovered what the Bible says about salvation, and how we can answer some common objections to the truth that Jesus is the only way to heaven.

One of the central verses supporting this truth is John 14:6: "I am the way, and the truth, and the life; no one comes to the Father but through Me." Jesus was preparing His disciples for His death, resurrection, and ascension. Just prior, Jesus said, "In My Father's house are many dwelling places; if it were not so, I would have told you; for I go to prepare a place for you. . . . And you know the way where I am going" (vv. 2, 4).

Thomas, one of Jesus's disciples, asked, "Lord, we do not know where You are going, how do we know the way?"

JESUS IS THE ONLY
RELIABLE GUIDE
WHO WILL LEAD
YOU OUT OF
THE WILDERNESS
OF THIS WORLD
INTO THE
PRESENCE OF GOD.

(v. 5). Jesus answered, in essence, "You want to know the way to this new place I'm going? I am the way. No one comes to the Father, to all the things I am preparing for you in heaven, except through Me."

One writer gave an illustration about a group of people getting ready to go on a guided trek through the mountains. They were disturbed to notice their guide wasn't packing any maps or even a compass. When they asked their guide about it, he just smiled. "Maps and compasses are not the way through these mountains," he said. "*I* am the way through the mountains."[1] That's exactly what Jesus was saying. He is the only reliable guide who will lead you out of the wilderness of this world into the presence of God.

What comfort do you take from Jesus's statement that He is the only way to heaven?

What will you do this week to help somebody else find the way of salvation?

Heavenly Father, thank You for providing a way of salvation that's simple enough for a child to grasp—yet beyond human comprehension! May I make choices every day that lead others toward your life-saving and life-changing grace.

.

Notes

Day 1 Christianity's Most Offensive Belief

1. Pew Research Center, "Few Americans Blame God or Say Faith Has Been Shaken Amid Pandemic, Other Tragedies," Pew Research Center, November 23, 2021, https://www.pewresearch.org/religion/2021/11/23/few-americans-blame-god-or-say-faith-has-been-shaken-amid-pandemic-other-tragedies/.

Day 7 Christians Are Being Outmarketed

1. Tim Adler, "MIPCOM: Disney-ABC TV Boss Anne Sweeney Says Television Will Get Even More Personal," *Deadline*, October 5, 2011, https://deadline.com/2011/10/mipcom-disney-abc-tv-boss-anne-sweeney-says-television-will-get-even-more-personal-179592/.

2. Ethan Cramer-Flood, "US Time Spent with Media 2022," Insider Intelligence, June 15, 2022, https://www.insiderintelligence.com/content/us-time-spent-with-media-2022.

Day 11 The Temptation of Universalism

1. Rob Bell, *Love Wins* (New York: HarperOne, 2011), 173–74.

Day 12 The Appeal of Pluralism

1. Pew Research Center, "The Changing Global Religious Landscape," Pew Research Center, April 5, 2017, https://www.pewresearch.org/religion/2017/04/05/the-changing-global-religious-landscape/.

Day 15 Why Exclusivity Matters

1. George Barna, "American Christians Are Redefining the Faith: Adherents Creating New Worldviews Loosely Tied to Biblical Teaching," Arizona Christian University Cultural Research Center, October 6, 2020, https://www.arizonachristian.edu/wp-content/uploads/2020/10/CRC_AWVI2020_Release11_Digital_04_20201006.pdf.

Day 21 The Real God

1. A. W. Tozer, *The Knowledge of the Holy* (New York: HarperCollins, 2009), 1.

Day 24 The Value of the Old Testament

1. J. I. Packer, *Knowing God*, 20th anniv. ed. (Downers Grove, IL: InterVarsity, 1993), 76.

Day 25 A False Dichotomy

1. Richard Dawkins, *The God Delusion* (New York: Houghton Mifflin Harcourt, 2006), 51.

Day 29 God's Holiness Reveals Our Sinfulness

1. Mark Buchanan, *The Holy Wild: Trusting in the Character of God* (Colorado Springs: Multnomah, 2005), 146.

Day 31 The Sinfulness of Man

1. John Ortberg, *God Is Closer Than You Think* (Grand Rapids: Zondervan, 2005), 37–38.

Day 33 Our True Spiritual Condition

1. G. K. Chesterton, *Orthodoxy* (New York: John Lane, 1909), 24.

Day 41 The Danger of the Wrong Approach

1. "In Re Air Crash at Dallas/Fort Worth Airport on August 2, 1985, 720 F. Supp. 1258 (N.D. Tex. 1989)," Casetext, accessed March 1, 2023, https://casetext.com/case/in-re-air-crash-at-dallasfort-worth-airport-2.

Day 42 The Intolerant Christ

1. Dorothy Sayers, *Letters to a Diminished Church* (Nashville: W Publishing Group, 2004), 4, 55.

Day 51 What It Means to Believe

1. W. H. Griffith Thomas, *The Christian Life and How to Live It* (Chicago: Moody, 1919), 30–31.

Day 53 A Variety of Lies

1. David Randall, "The Forgotten Victims: How the Titanic Tragedy Handed a Devastating Legacy to the People of Southampton," *Independent*, March 4, 2012, https://www.independent.co.uk/news/uk/this-britain/the -forgotten-victims-how-the-titanic-tragedy-handed-a-devastating-legacy -to-the-people-of-southampton-7466557.html.

Day 55 How the New Testament Answers the Exclusivity Question

1. *Real Time with Bill Maher*, episode 228, October 14, 2011, http:// www.hbo.com/real-time-with-bill-maher/episodes/0/228-episode#/.

Day 65 The Importance of Faith

1. John Bisagno, *The Power of Positive Praying* (Grand Rapids: Zondervan, 1965), 16.

Day 74 The Meaning of the Wrath of God

1. Leon Morris, *The Apostolic Preaching of the Cross* (Grand Rapids: Eerdmans, 1968), 35.

Day 80 Rejecting God's Revelation

1. Richard C. Lewontin, "Billions and Billions of Demons," *New York Review of Books*, January 9, 1997, https://www.nybooks.com/articles /1997/01/09/billions-and-billions-of-demons.

Day 82 The Basis of Idolatry

1. A. W. Tozer, *The Knowledge of the Holy* (San Francisco: Harper-SanFrancisco, 1978), 4.

Day 83 Natural Revelation Is a Test

1. Charles C. Ryrie, *Basic Theology: A Popular Systematic Guide to Understanding Biblical Truth* (Chicago: Moody, 1999), 37–38.

Day 100 Jesus Is the Only Way

1. William Beausay II, *Boys! Shaping Ordinary Boys into Extraordinary Men* (Nashville: Thomas Nelson, 1996), 23.

Dr. Robert Jeffress is senior pastor of the sixteen-thousand-member First Baptist Church in Dallas, Texas, and a Fox News contributor. He has made more than four thousand guest appearances on various radio and television programs and regularly appears on major mainstream media outlets such as  Fox News Channel's *Fox & Friends*, *Hannity*, *Fox News @ Night*, and *Varney & Co.*, as well as HBO's *Real Time with Bill Maher*.

Established in 1996, *Pathway to Victory* serves as the broadcast ministry of Dr. Jeffress and exists to pierce the darkness with the light of God's Word through the most effective media available. The daily radio program airs on more than one thousand stations. The daily television program can be seen Monday through Friday and every Sunday on more than eleven thousand cable and satellite systems, including the Trinity Broadcasting Network, where it has been the #1 viewed program since 2020. *Pathway to Victory* broadcasts reach all major markets in the United States plus 195 countries throughout the world. Additionally, *Pathway to Victory* ministers globally through podcasting and social and digital media. On each daily broadcast, Dr. Jeffress provides practical application of God's Word to everyday life through clear, uncompromised biblical teaching.

Dr. Jeffress is the author of more than thirty books, including *Perfect Ending, Not All Roads Lead to Heaven, A Place Called Heaven, Choosing the Extraordinary Life, Courageous, Invincible, 18 Minutes with Jesus*, and *What Every Christian Should Know.*

Dr. Jeffress graduated with a DMin from Southwestern Baptist Theological Seminary, a ThM from Dallas Theological Seminary, and a BS from Baylor University. In May 2010, he was awarded a Doctor of Divinity degree from Dallas Baptist University. In June 2011, Dr. Jeffress received the Distinguished Alumnus of the Year award from Southwestern Baptist Theological Seminary. He is also an adjunct professor at Dallas Theological Seminary.

Dr. Jeffress and his wife, Amy, have two daughters and three grandchildren.

Connect with Dr. Robert Jeffress:

 @DrJeffress   @RobertJeffress   @RobertJeffress